I0079234

To Silence

To Silence

Three Autobiographies

Subhash Jaireth

PUNCHER & WATTMANN

© Subhash Jaireth 2011

This book is copyright. Apart from any fair dealing for the purposes of study and research, criticism, review or as otherwise permitted under the Copyright Act, no part may be reproduced by any process without written permission. Inquiries should be made to the publisher.

First published in 2011.

Published by Puncher and Wattmann
PO Box 441
Glebe NSW 2037

http://www.puncherandwattmann.com

fiction@puncherandwattmann.com

National Library of Australia
Cataloguing-in-Publication entry:

Jaireth, Subhash

To Silence: Three Autobiographies

ISBN   9781921450426

I. Title.
A821.3

Cover design by Matthew Holt

Printed by McPherson's Printing Group

This project has been assisted by the Australian Government through the Australia Council, its arts funding and advisory body.

Australian Government

Australia Council
for the Arts

for HJ, KJ and MJ

Preface

The book is made of three monologues. I call them fictional autobiographies. The voices I have chosen are of three historically real figures: Kabir (1440-1518), Maria Chekhova (1863-1957) and Tommaso Campanella (1568-1639). By and large I haven't altered verifiable biographical facts but I have used creative instinct and imagination to make the voices narratively real and palpable. To infuse narrative drive to the monologues I have introduced a few fictional characters, such as Kalu Kasera in Kabir, Olga S and Egorushka in Maria Chekhova and Pietro, Abram Levi and Luigi Jolli in Tommaso Campanella. The existence of these characters can not be verified but their presence is highly probable and historically plausible. My research tells me that people like these did exist and might have played roles similar to those I have described in these imagined narratives. As far as possible I have tried to create real and authentic voices but the sensibility that drives the narrative is defined by the anxieties of our times.

Kabir

Kabir (1440 – 1518)

Kabir was a mystic poet of India influenced by Shaivite Hinduism, Tantric Yoga and Sufism. He is generally associated with the Bhakti Movement—a movement of religious and cultural reformation. The date and place of his birth are shrouded in mystery, as are the many circumstances of his life. His songs, couplets and verses were composed in a local dialect and widely sung during his time. Guru Nanak (1469-1539), the first Sikh Guru, compiled and edited more than five hundred verses of Kabir and included them in the Guru Granth Sahib, the holy book of the Sikhs.

Kabir was a weaver and hence metaphors related to weaving are abundant in his verses. In his songs he criticised both Hindu and Muslim orthodoxies and beliefs. He never wanted to be called a saint, but a saint he was made, with both Hindus and Muslims laying claim to his life and teachings.

The monologue begins a few months before his death.

Dear Swan, let's talk of the days gone-by
Of the place you come from and the place you call home
Of the place you paused to rest & left your soul behind;
The dawn has broken; it's time to say good-bye
No doubt or grief and of death no fear.
The blooming forest, the flood of fragrance—
All that splendour is a trap, and bliss, elsewhere.

[*Kabir-Vani,* Kabir]

I have renounced Kashi and returned to Maghar. They say I am mad to leave the holy city and perhaps they are right. It's the old age, they complain, that has clouded my judgment, my enduring sense of good and evil. They are convinced that I have erred and want to argue, hoping to change my mind, but soon give up unable to breach my stubborn silence. They think I am rude and perhaps a touch cruel. But I am merely tired and wish to remain quiet. My silence upsets them but I know that they harbour nothing but kindness for me, and I am sure very soon they'll give up and leave me alone to walk my lonely way to death. I also know that they feel concerned because they love me and love me more than I have ever loved them. This makes me sad because it should definitely have been otherwise.

I was born in Maghar and the moment I opened my eyes I saw the beautiful face of my mother. The cloudless sky was still and so was her face, round and bright like the full moon. The red shawl with yellow flowers had slipped off her head and her left hand was about to take out her—. No, I am wrong. This was later, much later. But something isn't right with my mind these days. It resists following my orders and plays tricks with me like an unruly monkey. I ask it to hop away and bring back a tiny glimpse of the very earliest past, but it always retrieves the same moon-like face looking from under the red shawl, as if trying to convince me that there isn't anything else worth remembering, that if memory has to start from somewhere, for me this would be the moment. The cunning beast has realised that my resistance is crumbling and is pleased to accept my capitulation. In return it rewards me with embellishments—the vision acquires sound, smell, and most important of all, touch. I express gratitude for this undeserved kindness and it leaves me alone to enjoy a few brief moments of indulgence.

13

The sound is that of a whistle but I am unable to resolve if it is caused by the wind or issues from her lips, but it's clear, so very clear. She is whistling a song without words. "Please sing me the words," I would ask her later and ask her again and again but she would refuse to sing the words. "Make your own to go with the tune," she would dare me, and laugh.

The smell is that of sweat and milk and of something else. Sometimes it reminds me of the hot cracked soil after the first shower. The summer brings frequent dust storms and the rain clouds only reluctantly come our way. But when they appear they surely bring rain and with it comes the smell.

The touch I find myself incapable to describe. It's more elusive than anything I have ever experienced. But touch it is—her finger gripped by a tiny fist. The finger, the fist and the memory of the first touch.

***

Yes, life begins with a touch and with a touch does it end.

And the end is not far. I can feel it tiptoe inside me—the footsteps, the cold touch of wet soles, cracked, rough and swollen. And it knows that I know and that I am not scared at all. At least not now; not like many years ago, when I was young and too busy to find a way to live in the penumbra of its omnifarious presence. Now I feel despondent that I have endured such a very long life. Why? I have often asked myself. Why so long? Why, so late? There is death everywhere and I have kept on living. How shameful, how utterly obscene!

Most children, I am sad to record, die at birth or within a year after. Their mothers often die before they have suckled the newborns. There is disease everywhere and no one to call for help. Only time, we have come to believe, has the power to heal or not to heal. Often death brings the ultimate relief. They pray, offer sacrifices, make promises, but to no avail, and in despair turn to magic, charm and outrageous witchcraft.

The rains fail to appear for years and people die with dreams of raindrops frozen in their listless eyes. The droughts usher famines and hunger sweeps through villages, emptying all signs of life. Even the rich are rendered helpless and die like ordinary beggars.

But worst of all are the wars. No misery is greater and no curse so stubborn and protracted. The tragedy is that both the curse and the misery are self-inflicted.

The other evening Kalu Kasera walked with me to Bakhira Tal. We sat near the pond under our favourite fig cracking dried seeds of watermelons from the last year's harvest. "I know the reason you have stopped weaving," he told me. I replied that I know that he knows and that it doesn't surprise me at all. We are friends and although he can work magic with everything of brass, he also manages to carve wonderful shuttles for my loom. He is older than me by several years and yet unlike me he wants to live and live, which is amazing because he carries within him a soul so deeply scarred.

He was nine and I had, so my mother tells me, just been born. Dehli, the great city in the west, with wonderful Kutub Minar and the great mosque, had been ravaged by the insatiable hordes of the Mongol Timur the Lame. Kalu calls him the *Langra* and doesn't utter his name without a curse.

Kalu was an apprentice in the workshop of a famous brass-smith who toiled for the Sultan and his *wazirs*. For three days he lay hidden under a pile of dead bodies. Four there were, he doesn't forget to remind me each time he tells the story. Three men and a little girl. The first thing he did after he had walked out of the city was lie in the waters of the Jamuna and wash and wash, but the smell of blood and rotten flesh wouldn't go. He doesn't remember how he managed to get to Kashi, but hasn't forgotten the three terrible nights he spent in Dehli scared by the soldiers of the 'great army' who had run amuck, slicing, chopping, killing everything that showed even a skerrick of life. All men, young and old, were killed. The old women were raped and the young, in particular the virgins, were taken away as slaves and concubines. Each soldier was ordered to bring to the barracks two severed heads as trophies. All animals except horses and elephants were slaughtered. The *Langra* was enamoured with elephants and took fifty of them back to Samarkand, the capital, not far from the serene Shahr-e-Sabaz, the green city, where the tyrant was born. The elephants carried stones for the Bibi-Khanym Mosque, adorned with the most beautiful azure dome in the world. Kalu doesn't believe me when I tell him that according to a traveller who had once come to visit Shaikh Taqui, the father of the lame tyrant had been so disheartened by the miseries of the world that he had retired to a Sufi monastery. When the tyrant had gone to visit him, he had reminded his warrior son that the world was a beautiful vase filled with scorpions. Kalu likes the quote and each time he remembers it his face lights up and an interminable laughter echoes through his whole body, making him breathless, and he begins to cough and spit.

Shaikh Taqui, may God bless his kind soul, told me that the Mongol had a kind and wise teacher by the name of Sayyed Barrakh who had persuaded him to become a Nusairi. "After devouring a hundred mice the cat decides to go on Hajj," Kalu whispers, and this time he doesn't laugh. He asks me to sing one of his favourite songs. I sing the song about the rain clouds because I too love that song:

> *Rain clouds gather and darken*
> *In the sky O Sadhu,*
> *The rain clouds gather*
> *And darken*
>
> *The string of clouds*
> *Has risen in the east:*
> *The rain comes down*
> *Rim-jhim, rim-jhim.*

Why do I like this song? "It's simple and sounds like rain," Kalu tells me and I whole-heartedly agree with him.

***

Kamaali has left her husband in Kashi and come with me to Maghar. She is silly. "I'll go back to him after I have seen you off," she explains in a measured voice. Her brother, the ever busy Kamaal, the glowing light of his mother's eyes, had come as well but returned after a few days, assuring me that he would send a messenger every few weeks and would do his best to be at my side when the moment arrives. Don't ask me why Loi, his mother, has refused to accompany me. She hasn't refused as such, but has found pressing reasons to stay behind. "While Kamaali looks after you, I'll look after her children," she has explained. "And then there is Kamaal, and his big family who need me. It is good to be needed, isn't it?"

There is no reason for me to disagree—she is needed and that's it. Should I have told her that I needed her too? Perhaps I should have, but I didn't and she must have concluded that she wasn't. Her decision to stay away sounds strange because she is so clever, perceptive and wise. The sense of being in the world she possesses is solely of her own creation and this, I know well, is the source of her confidence. If at times she has appeared unbelievably stubborn this isn't because she is selfish or arrogant but because she believes in her own sense of good and evil. I too have often benefited from her unwavering resolve and whenever I have felt lost I have instinctively looked for her, and fortunately she has always been there ready to do her bit. So now if she has decided to stay away from me, I have no choice other than to accept her decision and let her be free of my annoying presence.

But there is one thing which saddens me a little. Often at night as I try to catch a few peaceful moments of sleep I find her sitting beside me on the mat holding a fan in her right hand. I hear the fan swish, feel the breeze ebb and flow, and in the darkness of the small room I see her small face, which has grown even smaller with age, smile. But the smile fails to hide the fear she suffers from. I know that she fears for me, which is sad because I don't fear anything at all. The room is utterly dark and the few specks of moonlight dripping from the window are just enough to illume the silver nose-bud placed so precisely just above the edge of her left nostril. I raise my hand to touch the nose-bud but discover that the whole scene is nothing but an apparition. I soon stop thinking about sleep and once my mind is free and empty I hear the rhythmic hoot of owls. The two birds call each other and when suddenly one of them fails to respond my heart stops for a moment, waiting for the call. It soon follows and a strange pleasure begins to pulsate through my body. Just a few steps from death, I tell myself, and the body still finds strange ways of begetting pleasure. And then the sleep arrives and I forget for a few hours the anxiety with which I had waited for it.

The dreams I see these days are filled with sounds, as if the world at hand and far beyond has nothing of substance except sounds. I often feel that now more than ever it wants to initiate a heart-to-heart conversation with me, at the same time trying its best to remain invisible, as if scared that the vision will distort the purity of the tone.

But let me tell you about Chanda, the dear little daughter of Kamaali. The other day she took her first wobbly steps. I was sitting in the courtyard thinking about the pattern Kamaali wants me to weave. She has complained repeatedly that I have stopped weaving and perhaps that is why the songs too have stopped knocking at my door. I wanted to tell her that the absence of songs is caused by something altogether different: that these days my mind is enthralled exclusively by songs without words—no words and hence no anxiety about their meaning. Just pure sounds. Even the sound *Ra-am*, which had for so long remained glued to the most powerful of words, has become wordless; the flesh has peeled off leaving behind a tender rawness. But Kamaali is too busy to take note of my confused rambling. She wants me to weave a small sheet from which she will fashion a colourful dress for Chanda.

I enjoy watching little Chanda walk with Kamaali, her left arm raised and the tiny hand gripped tightly by her mother. But she is too eager and wants to break free and run, without knowing that her legs and feet are not strong enough for the overwhelming desire that makes her want to glide on the soft dung-pasted floor of the courtyard. She loses balance, sways like the stalk of a water lily, and slows down. And then I make an amazing discovery; the joy that just a minute ago lit her face has faded, replaced by fear. Has she already learnt the meaning of fear? I ask myself, and saddened by the knowledge I walk away.

But there is something else which grieves me even more and I don't quite know what to do about it. Perhaps it's time for me to tell Kamaali the truth: to tell her that although she is our most precious child she wasn't brought into this wonderful world by Loi and me. That Loi, her mother, didn't carry her in the womb and that we had tried our best to find the whereabouts of the stranger, perhaps a young widow in trouble, who had nourished her with her bodily juices.

It was just past midnight and Loi had got up to get a drink when she heard a cry. She opened the door and found a baby girl wrapped in a saffron sheet. Just a week before Loi had miscarried and perhaps that's why we had accepted the offering as a compensation. "Look what I have found," I heard her whisper and saw the girl for the first time. "Isn't she beautiful?" Loi asked. She indeed was—as beautiful as a piece of the lovely moon. "She is hungry," I wanted to say but Loi didn't need any prompting from me. She gave the baby her breast, looked at her with joy and wonder, and we decided to call her Kamaali—the little marvel.

I haven't asked Loi but at times I feel as if she might have already told Kamaali the truth or at least a version of it. Perhaps that is why I am so anxious and out of sorts. I suspect that she too has noticed the anxiety with which I sometimes look at her. But what difference would it make if I were to tell her the story, the way I remember it, again? No, it's not guilt. Not at all. Perhaps I want to test my memory, to see if it can recreate the far-away moments. Lately I have lost confidence in my memory. I have to ask Kamaali to remind me of the patterns which I used to weave without any effort. But this is not as bad as the inability to remember the verses which used to flow unhindered. No, even this isn't the real reason. I think I just want to thank her for being such a nice daughter. No, not to utter the words thank you but to make a gesture, and what can be more befitting than to tell her the story and acknowledge the boundless joy she brought us on that dark rainy night. Her brother Kamaal, the product of our own flesh and blood, is so different; his love for us is selfish and the arrogance with which he demands love from us in return is painful. But most irritating of all is the indifference he often displays towards us. Kamaali, perceptive as she is, hasn't failed to notice the displeasure resulting from her brother's behaviour, and perhaps that is why she tries her utmost to be kind to us. Yes, I should certainly tell her the truth. Tell her before it's too late.

I was ten or perhaps twelve when my mother told me that I wasn't her son. She was dismayed, even horrified, that despite Abbu's efforts I had suddenly stopped working on the loom. "The boy is going mad," she wouldn't stop complaining. "Doesn't eat or drink but sits the whole day in the corner shaking his head like a wooden marionette." I had told her that I wasn't sick and that I heard strange voices asking me to sing. She wanted to know about the songs, wanted me to sing them to her, and I did try a few times but nothing meaningful came out, as if by trying to utter them aloud I had drained meaning off them. It took me a while to learn to remember the words whispered to me by strange voices. I would repeat them, at first softly to myself and then a little louder and soon discovered that with each repetition they became more congruous; the excess was strained, leaving a residue—lean, light and luminous.

There is a carder in me, I told my mother, who beats on his bow day and night. She wasn't surprised because she knew how fond I had grown of Dadu Dhuniya who used to come every two or three months to thrash our cotton. He would fasten a bow to a peg in the wall, tie a cord in the middle of its string and attach a bigger bow to the cord. He would then hit the gut-string of the bow with a wooden club and the string would vibrate. He hated carding wool, which he thought gave an awful smell, but cotton he would card without any complaint. At first I hadn't taken much notice of him. He was a bit scary with his long grey beard and toothless mouth. Perhaps that is why I had at first tried to avoid getting close to him, but it didn't take long for the bow and the string to weave its magic; I was soon addicted to their persistent twang echoing in my enchanted ears and heart. For days after he had gone I would hear the gut sigh and sing.

But the singing gut was just the beginning because I soon discovered that the world both in me and outside was filled with sounds, and that I had merely to learn to keep my ears and heart open and it would stream in like a bubbling spring to play on me like a bamboo flute. Initially I used to shut my eyes to stay focused on the sounds, but gradually I was able to train my mind not to be distracted by the superfluity of the visual world. Soon the monkey-mind was tamed and the world, whenever I wanted, would transform into a perfect water bubble—thin, light and transparent.

I was thrilled by this power. It made me happy, content and strangely humble. But there was fear as well—the fear that the power that had so unexpectedly been bestowed on me would suddenly vanish, that the gods, angered by my arrogance, would punish me by withdrawing the invaluable gift. Yes, I was scared but the voice inside me wouldn't disappear. "There is a carder in you," it would whisper, "who knows every word you want to say. Let him card and wean. Don't hassle him. Just wait, be patient, and he'll make the verses fine and light like the muslin from Lakhnauti."

On that fateful day my mother had asked me to take a roll of fine yarn to the market to sell. "Try hard to get a good price," she had warned me repeatedly. I wanted to as well but then I saw a poor old beggar with a young boy of my age; the two had nothing on them and the people around them were laughing—even the monkeys had joined in to torment the poor creatures. I gave them the roll and walked away but didn't dare to go home. I didn't have the courage to face my mother. She would be furious I was sure and curse me no end. She would order me to pack my bag and leave as if I was not her son but a stranger. Was I a stranger? I guess I was. At least that's what she used to call me, whimpering and whining all the time.

I returned home after spending the night outside on the ghats and found her waiting for me at the door. She saw me and went inside. She didn't ask anything, didn't scream, didn't even raise her voice; she just looked at me and said, "You aren't my son and I am not your mother." At the time I didn't take much notice of what she said. I knew that she was hurting and wanted to hurt in return.

But it is true that I was rather different from the other so-called normal children of my age; unlike them I had shown little interest in the traditional occupation of my family—spinning, weaving and dying remained alien to me for a long time. Abbu didn't mind my lack of interest. "He will change," used to be his answer to Mother's frequent complaints. But I didn't change, turning stranger and stranger every day. She wanted me to learn the Qur'an by heart like a true *hafiz*, and recite the verses like a master *tajwid*, adding mellifluous tone and colour to their meaning.

I did eventually learn to recite the *Shahaadah,* but the word which spoke out most naturally of me was *Ra-am* and this annoyed my mother even more. For the son of a Muslim weaver I was behaving rather oddly—I had a Hindu guru and his name was Raamananda and the word he had given to me to chant wasn't Allah but *Ra-am*. I spent most of my days talking to sadhus and yogis; I didn't hate the idolaters and found nothing wrong in giving thanks daily to the river, the sun, the moon, the trees and every living or non-living thing which made life livable and exciting.

Abbu would tell me that I shouldn't worry about Mother because she would soon forget the disappointment, that she was angry because she loved me and wanted to protect me from the bad and the ugly. But she didn't forget and soon the neighbours, and through them the whole city, heard the unfortunate words and began to tell stories about her and me. Mother was shocked and so was Abbu but he knew that it was impossible to put an end to the stories. He tried to comfort her by saying that soon the people would find something else to talk about and leave us in peace. He asked her to be patient and pretend as if nothing untoward had been told and heard. As it turned out a two-headed elephant rescued us from further embarrassment.

The old man who first saw the elephant fainted and when he regained consciousness the elephant had disappeared. It was late at night and people assumed that the old man had either lost his mind or taken too much *ganja*. But the elephant reappeared two nights later in front of the Visveswara Temple just before the evening prayers. It tried to stroll up the steps but slipped and rolled down, scaring the crowd. The bells chimed and the drums bellowed and the elephant panicked, got up and fled, chased by an unruly mob. Three women and two young boys were crushed to death. The king of Kashi ordered his guards to look for it but they failed and gave up after a few months. Most agreed that it had probably drowned in the river but there were some who swore that the elephant was still alive and appeared and disappeared at will.

The stories about me and my mother were equally fantastic. The extraordinary ingenuity of some of them amazes me even now. According to one my mother was a Brahmin widow who was blessed by a yogi to give birth to a son. The yogi had made a mistake but the blessing was pronounced and hence she had to fall pregnant. However, being a widow she couldn't keep me and hence I had to be given away. So she placed me in a basket and left me afloat in the cool and calm waters of the Lahar Lake. Niru Julaha, my Abbu, and his wife saw the basket lodged within a thick growth of lilies and lotuses and took the basket and the baby home.

There were stories in which my birth was described as miraculous; one of them declared that I was born of lightning. According to the story it hadn't rained for three years and even the Ganga had begun to dry. All ponds, lakes and small rivers had emptied. The famine had begun, but then one day from nowhere the rains stormed in. It rained for ten, some say twenty, days. The Lahar Lake was full to the brim and that's when the lightning struck its surface with such a force that the water began to churn and rose sky high, and when it came down people saw a ladder and a woman walking down with a baby in her arms.

I am no saint, I tell them, but a poor julaha who doesn't know anything except weaving, and even the yarn that I happen to make is pretty ordinary. If occasionally I have composed verses and sung them aloud, the credit of that should go to the voices which echo in my mind and force me to talk in rhymes. My understanding of the world is very basic, derived from my own close-to-hand experience. I can't read or write and books, paper and ink don't mean much to me. In my lazy body sits a sluggish and at times unruly mind which either takes a while to figure out the shape of a neat thought or does its best to distract me from giving it an elegant expression. And the wisdom which some say speaks through my verses is equally modest and shallow. Perhaps that is why I am amazed that people have so readily come to believe that some divine and mysterious power has come to reside in me.

A few years ago I had gone to see the pond on the south bank of which, they say, the Buddha was born. The place is called Lumbini and is only a few hundred *kos* from Maghar. Mayavati, his mother, was tired and had decided to stop for rest and as she stood holding onto the branch of a large fig (I have seen and touched the fig as well) the child emerged from her right side. The pond, the water and a large fig—such an obvious setting for the mysterious and the miraculous to unfold. Why is water so significant in these tales? Take, for instance, Krishna; he is being carried in a basket across the Yamuna and the waters suddenly begin to rise, scaring Vasudev; but they rise just enough to touch the feet of the infant and recede ankle-high to allow Vasudev to walk across unharmed. True or false, these stories are beautiful and hence demand to be believed.

But what is beauty? How does it come to inhabit certain ideas, things and people? Take the song about the rain which Kalu likes so much. I like it too and know that if I were to take even a tiny word out, the whole song would lose its poise and harmony. So, it's an attribute of the song as a whole. But then why did the monk who came to see me the other day insist that beauty, like soul, enters the body of things and makes them beautiful? I didn't tell him that we were perhaps both wrong, because I have often felt that although beautiful things wither and perish, the sense of beauty inherent in them persists, like the memory of a cherished moment. I didn't tell him because I had guessed (how very arrogant of me!) his response—the true sense of beauty, he would have told me, is achieved not through engagement with the world but by turning away from it.

But why this sudden interest in the idea of beauty? Haven't I traversed the route many times and returned empty handed, unable to understand and explain the intricate patterns with which beauty and ugliness inhere the same worldly beings? That which is beautiful one minute turns ugly the next, the two as proximal to each other as the two sides of an *ashrafi* coin. But more astounding is the misapprehension that whatever is beautiful is necessarily good, and all cruelty and evil emanate from the ugly and the unseemly. We know well that this isn't true and yet we keep believing in this falsehood. It's desire, I would say, which clouds our eyes and corrupts our thoughts; we want the beautiful to be good and the good to be beautiful, forgetting that often the most healing syrup is obtained from the ugliest-looking plant and that the syrup itself is bitter to taste and foul to smell.

But I should leave these questions alone. It's too late for me to comprehend the complexity of the natural world—it's all too intricate and too confounding. I am not sure how many more lives I would have to live to see the light. Let it go, I should say to myself. Let it go.

I talk to Kalu about my misgivings. His response is unbelievably simple but surprising. At times I find in him the voice of Abbu, my kind and soft-spoken father. Kalu thinks like him, and for the most complex of questions his answer is often rather simple. No, not inane but profound because of its sheer simplicity. Like Abbu he tells me not to worry about the future, especially the future of your presence in the world after you are dead. "Take for instance the yarn you have weaved," he explains. "Once it is sold in the market what will become of it is beyond our control; part of it will be worn by a Brahmin and the other by a Kazi; yet one more part will become the shroud for the dead or the wrap for a newborn swinging in a cradle." And then he smiles, the same cheeky smile that makes me happy and nervous at the same time, and tells me about his dream— "there is no basket in the lake, no lotuses and lilies; the water is placid, heavy and grave. Suddenly a hand rises from the deep, unfolding; on the outstretched palm of this hand lolls an infant, ready to make his way into the world."

"I like this story. The bit about the hand. It's mysterious, beautiful and quite fitting for a weaver like you," he adds and smiles nonchalantly.

***

Kalu's son-in-law has come from Jaunpur. He is a stone carver and works for a master mason in the workshop of Bibi Raja. The queen has convinced Sultan Mahmud Shah to build a small but beautiful mosque. It's going to be her private mosque. It will be called the Lal Darwaza Masjid because the main entrance will be built in red sandstone. It will be located facing east. The main portal will have two more entrances, one facing north and the other south. These gates will lead to a spacious courtyard covered with a flat roof resting on strong but delicate columns. To go into the prayer hall you'll have to walk up a series of steps. "How big is the prayer hall?" Kalu asks. "Very big," answers the son-in-law. "Four big elephants can easily walk through it without bumping into each other." The prayer hall will have a zenana, an enclosure for women only, separated from the main hall by a latticed wall.

"It is going to be beautiful," he doesn't stop repeating. I want to know why but the revelation that the stones for the mosque have come from the ruins of the nearby Hindu temples distracts me, and when he tells us that this knowledge saddens him I feel sorry for him. "That is how it has always been," Kalu reminds him, "and that is how it will always be." I am astounded by the confidence with which Kalu, my good friend, speaks. But what amazes me even more is the advice he gives to his son-in-law: "Don't worry about these things. Your job is to cut and polish, and cut and polish you must with skill and application and forget about the rest, because the rest is nothing but thin air. Leave these matters to the rich and the powerful; let them fight their own bloody battles. The poor, my son, have no religion and the gods they need can do without mosques and temples."

"Where did you get these ideas from?" I asked him. "From you," he replied, reminding me of the exchange I had with the mullah of our mosque many years ago. "You were bemused by his loud calls for prayer," Kalu recounted, "and told him that it must be hard for him to climb up the minarets five times a day. He looked confused and you explained that he was wasting his time because the real mosque to which he called the believers was in him as well as in them, that if *Khuda* lived only in the mosque, how could he live everywhere. The real mosque, you told him, had not one but ten doors, and that he should turn his mind into Mecca and his body into Ka'aba. The poor man was so baffled by your riddles that didn't wait for you to finish and scurried away like a rabbit. He was scared of you and began avoiding you but you decided to camp outside the mosque and wait for him. Finally he came out of the mosque one day and sat down to talk. You heard him patiently and then asked him, 'Tell me, why do you shout so loudly from the minaret daily'?

'I say my prayers', he replied.

'I see', you said, 'your Allah must be deaf and blind like that poor beggar'."

Did I say that? I wanted to confirm, but I know that Kalu doesn't forget these stories easily; if my memory has turned into a sieve, his, I am sure, keeps every tiny speck in. "And what did I say to the pandit, my friend?" I asked him then. "Something quite similar," Kalu replied. "Get rid of your idols," you told him, "your beads, your holy thread. You didn't have them in your mother's womb. Search in your heart. There lives your *Ra-am*."

'Look at the pandits', you told me later, 'they pick up a stone in the street, scrub it clean, dab it with colour, drop a few marigolds and tell us that it has turned into a god. What sort of god is this, who can't even brush the flies off its face? And take their *linga*. They wash it daily with milk and water and bring it sweetmeats to eat. The god is hungry, they say. He is thirsty. No, the god is neither hungry nor thirsty. He doesn't need anything. Go and feed the poor beggars lining outside the temple gate."

"Don't you remember…" Kalu couldn't resist the temptation to recount other stories. Like a child he adores them and doesn't miss a chance to tell them, often embellishing them with details, the veracity of which I can't always corroborate. But his sincerity is beyond any doubt and the friendly devotion he displays towards me is incomparable. "Don't you remember how furious our poor mullah became when you confronted him that morning. He had, I remember it well, wanted to kill you that very instant. You were either too brave or too foolhardy. How can he be so audacious? I kept thinking about you. The unlucky creature asked you if you had been on the *hajj* to Ka'aba. You smiled and I knew from the smile that your reply would surely complicate the situation. You told him that you once departed for *hajj*, but had to return because as you were about to cross the bridge over our beautiful river you ran into God Himself. 'Where are you going?' He asked.

'To Ka'aba,' you replied.

'At whose behest?' He asked again, 'not mine I hope, because the Ka'aba you are going to is inside you'."

I know that my replies often baffle Kalu and I concede that he deserves better, but they reflect my own confusion. He is right when he complains that I despise the pandits and the mullahs in equal measure and they too hate me with passion, but for the commonfolk, I have nothing but the deepest love. Like children they are duped to believe what they shouldn't normally believe and they hate me because I refuse to participate in their silly games. No, hate perhaps isn't the right word. I think they are intimidated by my stubborn resolve to say whatever my humble heart bids me to say. To be honest, the heart I have isn't always humble; it's often arrogant and, to use their own word, 'mad'.

Mad and angry. Yes, I have on occasion lost my temper. I know I shouldn't have but it has happened and any suggestion that I am as human as anyone else shouldn't absolve me of such indiscretions. I remember once a pandit came to hear me sing. I was sitting outside the house in the shade of the large *neem*. The day was hot and sweaty and I didn't have the slightest desire to say even a single word. But he wouldn't relent and so I had to sing. Kamaali saw us and brought us water but the pandit wouldn't touch it, afraid that by touching the pot she was holding he would defile himself. You are stupid, pandit, I told him. Go away and don't show me your ugly face again. Go now otherwise I'll summon Mutiya, my lovely dog, to piss in your mouth. He was stunned by my angry response and Kalu, my dear friend, had to calm me down. I am sorry, I told Kalu. It was utterly puerile. But to be honest, what pained me most that day wasn't the insult thrown at me, but the hurt which my little darling Kamaali would have felt. I hope she has lost all memory of that sorry incident and if she still remembers it I hope she has found enough courage and grace to forgive the ignorant man.

***

A few years ago the news came about the passing away of Raamananda, my guru. I saw him only once in my life and that too when I was just a little boy. The young monk who brought the news told me of his painful death. He was quite ill and his mind, preoccupied by the body, mired with numerous afflictions, didn't want to let itself free. Hence he suffered. They say in the final years of his life he had grown fond of food and drink and had put on so much weight that even sitting up and walking had become too arduous.

The monk wanted to know if it was true that he was my guru. I said he truly was and still remains, because the real guru never dies. Each time you utter the word given to you by him the guru comes to life. He wanted to know more about him and I had to tell him the story he must have already heard a few times before.

I agree with Kalu, who has often told me that I must have been mad to venture alone the ghats that wintry night. Perhaps I was. I don't know, but desperate I surely was, searching in vain for the guru who could whisper the secret word to me. The night was dark and cold and to keep myself warm I had joined a group of sadhus sitting around a fire. The fire, however, soon died; there wasn't any wood, and dry leaves and cakes of cow dung didn't last long. The sadhus didn't complain, looked at each other and decided to lie down in a close huddle to keep each other warm. The ones who didn't want to sleep got up to walk to the burning ghats, hoping to spend the night near the pyres. I was scared that I would miss the guru and didn't want to sleep. I walked and walked that night, up and down the steps, from one ghat to the next. At times I didn't know if I was awake or walking in sleep. It was a strange walk—I would walk slowly, break into a short run and then stop, sit down, get up and walk again. Why? I had asked myself later and decided that it was because I was afraid to sit down; afraid that my mind would begin to question my resolve and soon lure me to go home and snuggle up to my mother—she would move aside and take me into her warm embrace and call the sweet sleep to come my way.

I was so busy walking that I didn't notice that a small white dog had joined me; she walked and ran with me and when I stopped she came close asking for a pat and a cuddle. I searched and found in my pocket a few bits of dried bread and lumps of sweet *gur*. The dog smelt the offering and devoured it immediately. She was hungry but didn't ask for more, as if knowing that there wasn't anything left in my pocket. But suddenly my legs gave up, refusing to follow my orders. My mind turned utterly blank. "Come on, lie down for a few minutes," I heard the voice whisper and I did lie down. It was a mistake because as soon as I stretched myself on the cold stony steps the sleep came over me. The dog didn't leave me; she drew near, offering me the beastly warmth of her body. I didn't mind and accepted the gift.

In the morning he stepped on her and not me. It was still dark and he was shivering after taking a dip in the cold water. The dog barked. "Hey *Ra-am*," he had snapped, angry to be confronted by a beast at such an early hour in the morning. I heard him growl, opened my eyes and touched his feet but he didn't take any notice and walked away, still cursing the dog. His name was Raamananda—the joy of *Ra-am*. "He will be my guru, the source of *Ra-am*—the blissful word," I whispered to myself and left the ghats.

That morning turned out to be unusually bright and sunny and as I rushed home through the bazaar I forgot everything about my little companion. She must have followed me for a while and then stopped, distracted by crows, cats, dogs and monkeys. I remembered her just before turning into our lane. I stopped and looked for her. "Mutiya," I had called out, "where are you?" She didn't come and I went home feeling elated and strangely sad.

I have told the story to Kalu several times and each time the clever old man (yes, he is very clever) has tossed at me the words of my verse in which I sing about the little white dog of *Ra-am*. He smiles and tells me that he knows the reason why the dog named Mutiya appears in one of my long-forgotten verses; forgotten by me but not by him at all. "I am Mutiya, the dog of *Ra-am*..." he sings the words wet with spit and laughs a deep throaty laughter. His whole body shakes and I begin to marvel at the uncanny ability with which he can reproduce each one of the verses he says I have composed. I believe him because I don't have any other way to check. There was a time when I used to sing them to check if all words were in harmony of sound and meaning, but slowly I have lost the desire to keep them preserved as they might have once upon a time appeared to me. There is no use, no reason and hence I have no interest to retrace the steps to the sweet spring from which they bubbled into existence—the primeval is but an illusion and what matters most is the flux and flow, the coming and going. Perhaps my desire to make the idea of flow universal itself is fallacious. The truth is simple; like birds the words fly away and if and when they return they never appear the same. Just sing them as they come to you and don't waste your time judging if you have uttered them before; most probably you have, most probably you will again.

No, it's not despair that has plagued my heart. The end is almost here and as I slowly try to relieve my mind of anxieties and apprehensions I begin to discover that the word beauty, which has so stubbornly nested inside my heart and mind, has acquired sorrowful intonations.

***

Yes, she was beautiful—the baby turtle I found in the pond. I was seven or perhaps eight (does it matter how old I was then?) and had for the first time discovered the joy of swimming. It took me a while to control my breathing and find the right rhythm between breathing and the movement of arms, legs and feet. Once I gained the confidence that the water wouldn't drown me, I began to enjoy it rippling around me, moving aside, giving me way and accepting me as if I was one of the many watery creatures who only know how to live and die in the water. At night, sleeping on the roof top and gazing at the starry sky, I would often feel that the sky was nothing but a bowl of dark silky water filled with amphibian constellations calling me to rise up and swim with them.

But that year the summer was unusually hot and dry and the pond had been reduced to less than half of its normal size; as a result we had to walk a fair way on the cracked patches of clay to reach the water. The clay was warm, littered here and there with shells, fish bones and large carcasses of dead cows, buffaloes and goats. I had been warned to be careful of the cracks where snakes often used to hide. At times you could hear them slither and hiss angrily.

I found her in one of the cracks, her neck stretched, trying hard to drag herself out. I looked at her and felt that she smiled. I leaned down to have a closer look and realised that she was stuck. I put my fingers in the crack to see if I could widen it. At first she tried to bite but after a few minutes drew back. I found a stick and inserted it inside taking care not to hurt her and then pushed hard; the clay around the crack began to crumble and within a few minutes the hole was big enough for her to squeeze herself out. She stopped for a moment and then sped fast in the direction of water. I ran after her and then she stopped exhausted and didn't move for a while. I heard two crows land not far from her, waiting for me to go away. But I didn't go. I picked her up. She was small, a little bigger than my palm. This time she didn't try to bite and didn't draw her neck in. She was beautiful; the upper surface of her shell was brown and green and the under-surface soft and very pale yellow. She didn't mind being turned over and prodded; I examined her paws and she didn't resist. I guess she didn't have any choice, but I am sure she knew that I wasn't going to hurt her. It is hard to believe but I still remember very clearly her beautiful eyes lined with dark wavy stripes on both sides.

I walked with her, feeling bad that I didn't have anything for her to eat. After reaching the water I put her down and realised that the crows had hopped along with me. She must have smelt water because I saw her getting ready to dash; her body tightened like an elastic string, she turned her head to look at me and then shot like an arrow towards the water. And then she was gone, leaving just a dusty trail on the clayey surface.

I didn't tell anyone about her, not even mother. She was mine and would remain so forever.

***

Kamaal, my ever-busy son, has brought a *nassakh* with him. Ashraf, he tells me, is a professional scribe valued highly by all the rajahs and nabobs. Kamaal wants me to dictate the verses to him so that he can write them down on sheets of paper, so smooth and white that although I have touched them many times I am still not convinced that one could or should write on them.

Ashraf's uncle is one of those clever *Kagadi Musalmans* who make excellent paper. I am curious and want to know how such a delicate thing is made. Ashraf understands my eagerness and without much asking begins to describe the process. I listen carefully trying to remember the details but soon lose track. Luckily he doesn't notice and I am able to convince myself that it must be quite an arduous task to produce sheets of such a good quality. He doesn't fail to remind me that the work requires patience and lots of practice to master the use of poisonous substances often corrosive and malodorous. I believe him when he informs me that women perform the most delicate of jobs—the spreading of gruel onto the screen to obtain a thin uniform filament of pulp. In his description I hear names of strange substances and places—the gunny bags from Govindpur, the *sajikhar* (carbonate of soda) from Bikaner, quicklime from Jhansi and soap from Nagpur. It takes them twenty to thirty days to turn the shreds of gunny bags into sheets of paper, some of which can fetch up to ten *tankas* for a batch of hundred sheets.

Kamaal wants Ashraf to stop talking and get on with the job. It doesn't take him long to notice that my queries are nothing but a ploy to delay the inevitable. It is dangerous to row two boats at the same time, I warn him but he doesn't listen. "Not at all Abbu," he argues with a glint in his eyes. "An extra boat is always handy—if one sinks the second is there to save you." We both know that he has never rowed a boat in his life and that his sole aim is to contradict me. I want him to leave me alone but can't find the resolve to tell him so. His persistence irritates me and the zeal with which he wants to finish the task baffles me no end.

30

In the evening when his sister is busy cooking he whispers to me the details of his clever plan. He is worried, he tells me, that some enterprising songsters have started making money by singing my verses in bazaars and fairs. There is nothing wrong with that, I assure him, and I don't consider them to be my songs any more.

He ignores my remark and I know that he thinks my attitude in these matters is utterly impractical, but what irritates him the most is that some of these charlatans (yes, that's the word he uses for them) have begun to append my name to their own insignificant and pitiful compositions. He wants to protect my name he repeats again and again but we both know that he is also interested in making money. "Isn't that so?" I ask him. He looks at me and his answer—"not for me but for Mother"—doesn't sound convincing at all. I am aghast at the wickedness of his plans but I know that he won't leave me alone. I will have to acquiesce. A few years ago I would have told him to go away or would have myself walked out but now I am too tired to mount any credible resistance. I hate myself for feeling so helpless.

After two days of cajoling and haranguing I give up but he is forced to make a vital concession—that the writing will happen in the presence of my dear friend Kalu.

On the morning of an auspicious Tuesday we take our seats in the shade of the fig outside the house. I am surprised to see Kalu so excited. He ignores my apparent indifference and keeps himself occupied with his two grandsons who have come with him to witness the show. I have to confess that although I am an unwilling participant in this enterprise I do like the meticulous way Ashraf goes about his job. He opens a small bundle and separates a quarter of the lampblack carefully and pours it into a small clay pot; from another small packet he retrieves a few blobs of Arabic glue and dissolves it in lukewarm water and the mixture is added to the pot. The mouth of the pot is tightly shut and shaken thoroughly for a few minutes. He dips a stick in the pot and examines the colour. From the smile on his face I conclude that he is happy with the result. The next step is to prepare the pen; he takes a reed out of a bag, finds a knife and fashions a flat edge sliced at an angle. He leaves the pen in the inkpot and without losing any time assembles a small wooden writing desk. But he isn't ready to start writing yet. "I have to train my hand," he explains and fetches an old rough sheet and begins to write, pausing after each letter. The exercise goes on for a few minutes. Once he feels that his hand has acquired the necessary steadiness he announces that he is ready.

A brand new sheet of paper is placed on the desk and he looks in my direction, and we both notice that everyone else is waiting for me to speak. I wait as well but the words fail to appear. I panic. I have lost them, I tell myself, lost them forever. As always Kalu steps in at the right moment, saving me from further humiliation.

"Dear swan," he starts, "let's talk of the days gone bye."

"Not so fast," Ashraf reprimands him. Kalu takes no offence. He understands the seriousness of Ashraf's task.

It takes us an hour to dictate the whole song. Once the writing is complete, Ashraf's young son spreads a handful of dry sand on it; "to soak and dry the extra ink," he explains.

"Do you want me to read it out?" Kamaal asks me and doesn't wait for my reply. He starts slowly, reading at first each word separately and then re-reading the whole verse again. We all listen. Kalu asks him to read it again. I keep quiet. Kamaal ignores Kalu's request and waits for me to say something. Like Kalu I am confused. We both know that something strangely untoward has happened to the words he had an hour ago so earnestly dictated. Why do they sound so different?

"What's wrong?" Kamaal asks and from the expression on his face I conclude that he too has spotted the difference.

Yes, what's wrong? I ask myself.

Kalu takes the sheet from Kamaal and shows it to me and we both gaze at the dark black marks. They aren't all dark. Their colour lightens gradually, reminding me of the spot where Ashraf dipped the pen in the inkpot. I like the curved shapes interspersed with straight lines, topped with umbrella-like domes and squiggles, some sitting alone and others joined with a straight line at the top.

"Where is the word 'swan'?" I ask Ashraf and the shape pointed to me seems a little familiar, particularly the first letter capped by a squiggle that reminds me of a flattened sickle with a black dot in the middle. It looks like a boat, I want to ask Kalu but change my mind. Kalu doesn't need to be asked; he reads my mind as if it is his own and agrees that the word with a boat-like shape does bear some resemblance with the real swan. All of a sudden a strange quiver runs through my body and as I begin to recount the words which Kalu had dictated I discover that they have acquired shapes similar to the one I had just a minute ago seen on the sheet. An uncanny thought flashes in my mind and I tremble with both fear and excitement; there is, I think, a white sheet of paper hidden inside in me on which an unknown 'Ashraf' has scribbled the shapes without ever telling me about them. How exciting, I mumble.

"Did you say something?" Kalu asks me but I rudely ignore the question because I feel that the thrill that I experienced just a moment ago is turning into fear. Why fear? Of what? Of the scribe, I whisper to myself—the invisible scribe living inside me. The idea troubles me but before I can find a credible explanation to assuage my heart another quite extraordinary revelation overwhelms me.

I take the sheet from Kalu to examine it closely.

"What's wrong? Why won't you tell me?" Kalu can't wait anymore.

"The thing is," I start unsurely, still guessing the final shape of the thought that has slowly begun to emerge, "on Ashraf's sheet the words flow continuously from left to right moving like a coiled snake. No gaps, no stops and no interruptions. There is no place for a breathing space there, no marks to tell you that you need to pause for a moment here and to accelerate there. The shape in which this song appears in my mind is very different—a sort of ladder painted in the middle of the sheet; steps of the same length alternating—a short step followed by a long one and thus on and on. There is a vertical bar standing at the end of each line telling me that I have to pause for a moment—to catch breath and to regain balance. Yes, now I know why silence is so important for the song to work its magic."

Ashraf is happy to copy the song again but Kamaal doesn't want to waste paper and time, yet he knows that I have made up my mind and he will have to relent. Ashraf on the other hand doesn't need convincing. He quickly takes out a new sheet and asks me the place from where to begin. This time when Kalu dictates I prompt him to pause at the right moment. The pauses define the length of the step or the line in the ladder. The finished song, we soon discover, has seven lines; the first line is the shortest, almost half the size of the rest. At the end of each line there are bars—single and double alternating: two bars denoting a longer, almost two-fold duration of the pause. Ashraf is very pleased with the result; its symmetrical shape delights him.

Kamaal doesn't like the blank space left around the written song. He is irritated that it will cost him more paper and hence more money. But finally when he agrees to read the song scribbled on the paper, the faint smile on his face tells me that he too has grasped the subtle beauty resulting from the balanced shape of the song.

However, he doesn't hesitate to remind Ashraf that he wants him to spend less time on each song. His tone impairs the joy we have so unexpectedly experienced. We want him to keep quiet and allow us to savour every moment. But the moment doesn't last long because we soon notice that a flock of pigeons has landed on the fig. We all hear the flutter, the throaty calls and unruly ruction. We look up and at that very moment one of them decides to bless us with a lavish chunk of liquid droppings. The droppings miss us but land directly on the sheet with the copied song, and before Ashraf or his son can understand what has happened most of the writing is smudged.

Kamaal is understandably annoyed and we feel sorry for him. I turn my face away to hide the smile which would have angered him even more. Luckily I manage to reign in the urge to lecture him on the transient nature of the written word. I am sure in a few days when he has calmed down he will recognise that writing isn't the most reliable of means to preserve the spoken word; that both ink and the paper which it stains are as, or perhaps even more, perishable as any living creature. That although passing from mouth to mouth the spoken word alters its sound and intonation, the alteration is not a curse but a blessing in disguise. In the end it doesn't matter who is the first to utter the words of a song; the idea of origin and of ownership is not only tenuous but of very little significance. No one can lay claim on the words because once they have been uttered they become common to us all; we need to have patience to hear them with love and to pass them on to others with grace and humility. Only then can one hope to make the words live forever.

***

The time has finally come. The wait is over. Just a few more days and I will be gone and there won't be any more pain to endure. At times the pain is so intense that I cease to feel anything, even the pain itself. Like a white swan I flap my wings and break into the blue span of an endless sky; for a moment it seems pure ecstasy. But it lasts only for a moment, because soon the consciousness returns and I am engulfed by a new wave of pain. Why have you forgotten me, my *Ra-am*, my guru, my blissful Karim? Why can't you end this torture? I am tired and you know that I have done my best to endure it. It hasn't been easy and Kalu knows how at times I have cried like a helpless child. Yes, blessed are those who die peacefully unscathed by pain and suffering.

Three days ago I caught a cold and knew that it would soon induce asthma that my feeble lungs would find hard to tolerate. Since then three more days have passed and it feels as if they have shrunk to the size of a tiny bag able to capture only a fistful of air.

I have suffered from asthma my whole life. I was seven when I had my first attack. My Abbu wasn't surprised. "He is the son of a weaver," he told my mother. He wanted me to learn to live with it as he himself had to. The tricks were simple—to refrain from eating greasy food, to avoid dust and strong odours and when the winter came to try to keep the body neither very warm nor very cold. However my mother had other ideas. She was a fighter and would fight the dreaded affliction with all her might. She would learn whatever there was to be learnt about herbs and potions and devise a credible regimen to strengthen my body and lungs. Her passion was matchless and her will to help me indelible. There were times when she would disappear from the house for days and return with bundles of foul-smelling roots, seeds, flowers and stems. As always she gathered around herself a small group of young girls who helped her prepare the extracts, mixtures and powders. She turned into a *hakeem-bibi*, giving free consultations, diagnosing ailments and afflictions and dispensing drugs with amazing authority and confidence. Her favourite used to be an extract of *tulsi*; she would boil the leaves on slow heat and leave the liquid to cool overnight. The extract was bitter and she would add a few drops of honey to make it drinkable. Once, a fierce-looking yogi brought from the mountains a plant called *vasaka* and told her that the brownish roots with pea-size knots were very potent in healing many afflictions of the lungs. But he had warned that the extract should be kept away from the children and young women because like *ganja* it would surely make them go wild.

It's the *vasaka* with which Kalu treats me now. He mixes the dried leaves with a little bit of *ganja* and coaxes me to take a few puffs. I am amazed at my own stubborn resistance, at my resolve to say no, and deny my body the briefest of respites. In the end I give in—just to make him happy, I whisper to myself. How vain, I think soon after, shamed by the conceited thought. That's why I suffer, I repeat again and again: so close to death and yet so focused on myself. Let it go, I should say; let it vanish once and for all. O my stubborn mind, why are you still so preoccupied with the well-being of this perishable body? Why do you wait for the snippets of pleasure that follow the slightest alleviation of pain?

The warm puffs soothe my throat and although I don't feel any loosening in the lungs the pain recedes and I am able to catch a few hours of sleep. But no, it isn't sleep at all. Just a descent into a deep well; the water quivers and like a leaf

I bob up and down, up and down.

Sleep. What a sweet word! I don't remember anymore the joy of uninterrupted sleep. It's gone. Whatever it is, sleep or emptiness, I experience it sitting down, leaning against the wall. I don't complain and accept whatever comes my way. Lying flat on the ground has become impossible. There was a time when I used to lie down on my left side and sleep breathing from one lung, but now it looks as if that too has turned thin and flat like Kamaali's little *chapattis*.

Luckily it's neither very cold nor hot during the day and the nights are very pleasant. Kamaali has arranged the mat along the side wall and I sit most of the time looking through the small window. I feel sad to watch her suffer because of me. She touches me and I sense from the touch the pain she herself must be going through, but her touches are short and swift as if she is afraid that she may inadvertently hurt me. Why? I want to ask. She shouldn't. This body can't feel any more hurt. She shouldn't cry either. Don't fret my dear little swan, I want to tell her. I have lived a happy life and your presence in it was a true joy. Hence there is no need to tear yourself apart. Don't waste your time sitting by my side. Your little Chanda needs you more. Please go out and play with her. Hearing you giggle together brings me immense pleasure. Yes, don't waste your love and compassion on an old man. That he is your poor father doesn't matter anymore. Try, my dear, to initiate the process of forgetting. It has to begin now otherwise it will be too late. You don't want me to hang like a dark shadow in your memory. No, I don't tell her anything at all because I know that she would be hurt. I guess it's her fate as well—to witness my suffering and suffer herself.

My suffering is of my own making. I am being punished, I know it well. I have erred, I know it too, and have been guilty of many iniquitous deeds; but most of all I feel ashamed of the unbelievable arrogance of my youthful years— the stubborn and at times almost blind belief in my own indestructibility. How stupid I was, how hypocritical! The songs I sang were beautiful, I concede, but I had doubts about the truth they preached. I was playing games the way my *Ra-am* is playing with me now. Yes, I do deserve the pain I am going through, hoping against hope that it will finally cleanse me of my past blemishes. The soul will fly away like a luminous white swan, unsullied and innocent, and vanish forever leaving behind just a faint trail. I can see the swan. Here it comes. It has landed and look, it's about to take off.

On most nights Kalu sits with me and talks continuously, although I often feel that it's not him, because it would be impossible to talk without a break. There

36

must be something else behind this continuous humming. I guess his words, after he has stopped talking, reverberate like the string on the bow of Dhuniya the carder, ebbing and flowing in the air.

What was his name? Why can't I remember it? I should ask Kalu, I decide but when I ask, his answer confuses me even more. The name Chogyam sounds familiar and I force myself to focus more ardently, and after many attempts I realise that Kalu is telling me the tale of the Buddhist monk who came to Kashi to see me. He had travelled from Tibet and had brought with him a herb called Ma-huang. "It grows on the high plateau with little or no rainfall," (It's Kalu's voice again). "The shrub has a long narrow stem with tiny leaves. The most beneficial of plants has red leaves, yellow flowers and tiny nodes on the stalk. The plant loves the sun. Perhaps that is why the extract prepared from the leaves is warm and soothing. The seeds are good as well; they are dried and roasted and a paste of the powder is used to treat the sick." The monk too preferred the paste and had told me to chew it: "put a small portion on the tongue, roll it in the mouth and allow it to dissolve slowly."

I like the paste; it pushes me into a state of trance, traversed by a continuous stream of weird dreams. I also hear voices, mostly modifications of Kalu's. But I also detect a female voice; I suspect it's that of Lallesvari, dancing and singing, her body covered in nothing but grey and black ash, her long hair swaying, her feet sliding and slapping. I feel dizzy, want to sit down, shut my eyes and listen to the sound of the song bouncing around me. I hear it enter me and I too begin to sing: "Whatever name you bear, O Lord, take away from me—the sick woman—the sickness of the world…" Soon the ash-covered figure disappears, leaving only the voice. "Did we ever meet her?" I ask Kalu. He ignores my question. Why? Doesn't he remember her anymore? It can't be. His memory is so immaculate, so incorruptible. I know that like others he too must have been intimidated by her. Who wasn't? Even I was in the beginning but then I soon understood that I was afraid of my own desire; yes, for her and for her immaculate beauty, enhanced manyfold by her desire to show and give. I was wrong because the pleasure she wanted to give and share was of another kind—the one which you begin to experience through your body but it soon transcends it, transporting you to other realms where body turns into thin air. Was it death?

"You are dying," I hear him whisper.

"I know I am but so what?"

"You need to think about the future."

"Whose?" I ask, "Is there any after I am dead?"

"I know," I hear him laugh and he pleads with me to be serious.

"What can be more serious than death?"

"The people we leave behind." His answer puzzles me at first but I soon grasp the meaning of the subtle gesture. "They know you are dying," he speaks, "and have gathered outside waiting for the news. They are agitated and want to break in—to look at you, to touch your feet and if possible to grab a morsel of the soil you are lying on. But most of them have come to claim your body—the Hindus want a cremation, the Muslims a burial and no one is ready to give an inch. I am worried, scared about Kamaali and Chanda. What should I do? Tell me. What should I do?"

Kalu is right. I can hear the crowd but what I hear doesn't seem to make any sense. I try to speak but the words I utter remain unheard even by me. I try hard, and exhausted by the effort I shut my eyes. Immediately a darkness descends—the water is raven black, the touch silky but there is no air to breathe. I am drowning fast when suddenly I spot a small turtle, the same beautiful turtle of my childhood. It is swimming in my direction, its neck stretched out, the eyes shining through the slimy ooze, and as I extend my hand to touch it, the world suddenly comes alive.

I see Kamaal and Kamaali sitting with Kalu, looking and waiting. "Where is Chanda?" I want to ask. I want to touch her little face, her hand, her tiny tiny toes.

"Yes, that's what we'll do," I find Kalu leaning down beside me trying to say something to me. I can see the lips move, the wrinkles quiver, the moustache twitch, but I can hear only whispers. "Kamaal will go outside and talk to the leaders of the two groups and beg them to go away to let you breathe your last in peace. He'll tell them that once you are deceased the leaders of the two groups will get a chance to decide about the body. It won't be easy, I know, but Kamaal is clever—he'll find a way to convince them to leave and come back in the morning. And once they are gone we'll whisk you away. I have already arranged a cart with two pairs of healthy bulls and before the dawn breaks we'll be out of their reach."

"Do you remember the Buddhist monk who told us about the mountain with a cave? We'll take you to the mountain. Yes, the journey will be hard but is there any other way to escape the fury of an angry mob? It will have to be pacified, bribed perhaps by a neat story—unworldly but believable. We'll leave on the floor a little mound of moist marigolds covered by a white sheet. In the morning Kamaal will call in the crowd and unveil before them the marigolds and tell them about the miracle that occurred at night in the house; that you didn't die as we all die but rose to the heavens alive, in body and flesh, bequeathing them the fresh marigolds as the blessed remains; one half will go to the Hindus to be released in the holy Ganga and the rest will be given to the Muslims to be buried near the western edge of the pond under the shade of the big fig; this way they will all receive whatever they have come to claim. The miracle will save the day and save us and them as well."

***

Isn't it a wonderful night? I am lying in a bullock cart. It rocks and rolls. The wheels squeak, the bulls snort, the bells jingle, the tails swish and swash. The rhythm soothes. It brings in waves of sweet slumber which only last a few minutes. I open my eyes to peek at the dark sky and shut them again; the stray stars enter my eyes and remain blinking inside. I carry my own starry sky, I whisper to myself, and then just to check that it wasn't a dream I open them and find Kalu sitting near my feet, smoking a pipe. A blanket covers his head and with each suck his face lights up. He sucks, sighs and coughs; I hear him gather the phlegm, roll it into a lump and spit.

The night sky is dark and empty but for a white speck floating like a tiny feather; at times it comes so close that it begins to resemble a white swan. Its long neck has patches of brown, the bill glitters and the black knob at its base augments the glow. It beats its large wings softly. My mother used to walk like this, the hem of her sari making the same soft rustle. Where is she now? Look, the swan has flown back—turned into a small white speck. Why is it playing tricks with me? Why can't it come and sit with me? Not at my feet but right here near my head. Now even the speck has disappeared; I can't see it anymore but the sound of the flapping wings continues. The sound floats on the breeze—it's cold, soft and moist like the morning dew. Someone is touching me.

Who is this walking over me? The feet so small, like those of Chanda's, her silver anklets tinkle and then she giggles and calls Baba … Baba … Baba … I feel her hand touch my face. Baba … Baba … Baba …

I know where Kalu is taking me. The monk who explained the healing powers of Ma-huang also described the way the folks in his village farewelled their dead. "The dead are carried to a flat top of a high mountain," I hear him speak, "and are left on the ground unrobed. After saying the prayers the villagers depart, leaving the eldest son behind in the nearby cave; he has to keep watch and wait for the vultures and other wild animals to arrive. It only takes a few hours for the body to be consumed."

"Sounds cruel," I remember Kalu remarking.

"Cruel it may be, but fair," I hear myself reply, "that's what I would like for myself."

The cart has stopped, the bulls are unharnessed. I can't see Kalu anymore. He must have gone to wash himself. Perhaps that is why the white swan has decided to come and sit with me. It's perched on my right shoulder. I savour the touch of the wings which smell of the summer rain. I feel it burrow its bill under my arm. It tickles and I want to laugh but can't. It leaves my shoulder and comes to lie down with me, its head resting on my stomach. I hear its heart beat; the breathing is soft, assured, unperturbed. I feel light and buoyant, almost like a feather.

"Let us go," I hear it speak. The wings flutter.

"Let us go," I reply.

Maria Chekhova

Maria Pavlovna Chekhova (1863-1957)

Maria Chekhova was the younger sister of Anton Chekhov, the famous Russian writer. After finishing her education she became a teacher and taught history and geography in a girls' school in Moscow. She also studied painting and wanted to take it up seriously. The celebrated Russian landscape painter Isaac Ilyich Levitan (1860-1900), a close friend of the Chekhovs, provided guidance and encouragement.

After Chekhov's death in 1904, Maria lived in the house in Yalta where she organised the Chekhov House-Museum. In 1922 she was made its Director and spent her life working there. She also compiled, edited and published most of Chekhov's letters.

Maria Chekhova was friends with many well-known Russian writers including Ivan Bunin (1870-1953), who was awarded the 1933 Nobel Prize, and Aleksandr Kuprin (1870-1938). One of the two Olgas in the monologue is Olga Knipper (1868-1959), the well-known actress at the Moscow Art Theatre whom Chekhov married in 1901.

The monologue is set in Chekhov's house in Yalta. The year is 1953.

Masha! Make haste and come home. There is nothing to eat, the flies are sickening. The mongoose has broken a jar of jam.

[From Anton Chekhov's letter to Maria Chekhova, June 1891]

"You ask me, dear Olechka, if I have heard the news. I certainly have. Who hasn't? And it's such good news. *Slava Bogu* he is dead. Such a long and frightful wait! I am happy, and both you and I can be sure that Anton would have been happy as well. At last the tyrant is dead …"

I didn't continue with the letter. Instead I wrote a short 'everything over here is fine' sort of letter. I wrote about the spring rain, Anton's rose beds in the garden and the leaking roof in his study, meaning I would have to call in someone for repairs. I told her that she should look after herself; that we are now both old and frail and need to deal with joys and sorrows in a measured way; that I am looking forward to her visit in June; that although I am suffering from mild but persistent headaches, by then I should be all right, and ready to welcome her.

She will be intrigued to find the date 6 March at the bottom of the letter, just above my name. The drawing of a smiling face beside it will certainly amuse her, and I know that she'll understand its meaning.

I am happy that Stalin is dead. Who isn't? It is the only death that has made me happy. Happy is perhaps the wrong word. Relieved would be better. I thank God that we, both Olga and I, have come through the terrible times unscathed, with our hands unsoiled and our souls untarnished: that to save our lives we haven't had to put someone else's life in danger, and that we have lived truly and honestly, as Anton would have wanted.

I know it's harsh, but I am glad that my brother died without facing the Revolution, the Civil War and the dreadful Great Patriotic War. I am not convinced that he would have survived the experiences. Yes, he had been to Sakhalin and seen the convicts in that dreadful prison, but that was nothing compared with what followed after the Revolution and the purges. The Famine would have broken his heart, particularly discovering that it was mostly man-made and driven by a desire to take revenge and to make the poor poorer and more miserable.

Perhaps that's why I'm surprised that I have survived. Why? Because I am a woman, some would say. "You had your Anton," others (like Olga) often argue.

She should know. She had her Anton as well. Yes, he has kept me alive, he and this God-forsaken house, this unbelievable nightmare, this burdensome cross I have been forced to carry. I'll be glad to be rid of it, then I won't have anything to worry about, nothing to keep safe and secure, nothing to look forward to; just peace and quiet. "I endure, and will endure until the day I breathe my last," I say, and if I sound like *Uncle Vanya's* Sonya, I don't mind at all. Isn't there a Sonya in each of us?

Olga wouldn't have survived if she and Anton had managed to make a little Pamfil. That's the name Anton had chosen for his unborn son. A little half-German, he used to call him. He always wanted to be a father, always, and yet he left it too late. He should have found a wife earlier, when he was young and healthy; my dear friend Lika was more than ready to give him one. He was silly, chasing women, having affairs. Why was he so unsure of himself?

A few years ago I asked Olga about the miscarriage. My question upset her and she started crying. I shouldn't have asked. I was rude and perhaps a bit cruel too. But to hurt her wasn't my intention. We are sisters-in-law, and for the first few years it was rather difficult to share Anton with her, knowing full well that Olga as a wife had more claim on him. Since Anton's death, however, we have come to appreciate one another's loss and grief. We have learned to live with each other.

It was fifty years ago, and she still remembers the fall clearly. "I was rehearsing Gorky's *The Petty Bourgeois* and Nemirovich-Danchenko wouldn't leave me alone; I had to run up and down those awful stairs. No wonder I collapsed! In no time it was all done, finished forever." She need not have told me. I knew the story well, the tragedy and its aftermath. Anton had shown me her letters. He was upset by the miscarriage and saddened by the pain Olga had to suffer. But there was something else as well, more troublesome and heartbreaking. I could see it from his face, from his eyes, the way he would look away. He was a doctor, after all, a fairly good obstetrician, and the telegram from the surgeon who had treated Olga hadn't removed his doubts. The fact that he wrote a note to him asking for details would have been an ordeal in itself. He had always suspected something going on between Olga, the leading actress of the theatre, and the Principal Director, although the Director was, so they say, happily married.

But who am I to blame Olga? Don't we all have something to hide and be ashamed of? I am certain Anton never told Olga anything about Karatygina. She was much older than he and had very little talent. *Zhuk*, he used to call her.

Imagine sleeping with her and calling her names afterwards. Anton had his blind spots too.

I know them well, the blind spots. They are there in his letters. Hidden but I know how to find them. Yes, the blasted letters are the real problem. Thousands of them. To me he wrote at least a few hundred, and I didn't leave a single one unanswered. I even scribbled a few extra of my own. He loved writing letters and found time to write to so many people, and most of them never failed to write back. Letters and more letters! They are all here with me and I have read them all. Anton was lucky he didn't have to read the letters addressed to me; some of them are more revealing than the ones sent to him. That's how I've come to know more about him than I ever wanted to. This, I think, is my real problem, my life-long predicament.

The author of a good novel, Anton would say, knows more than the protagonists themselves: their past, present and future. Sometimes it feels as if I too have become an author of Anton's novel-like life, knowing more about him than he could have possibly known. He is dead, but his life as a character continues, because stories, as he used to say, never end; in fact, you seem to keep on writing the same story again and again. There is a change here, a change there, but the story remains essentially the same.

Some of his friends had asked me to destroy their letters to him and I unwillingly complied, but before getting rid of them I couldn't keep myself from reading what they said. Most of my life I have spent editing the letters, compiling notes, introductions and explanations. I'm pleased that they have been published, at least most of them; the rest have been carefully filed and put away. It would have been easier if I hadn't been compelled to read them all; the burden of knowing so much is hard to endure. Now I know why ignorance can sometimes be such bliss.

***

Olga left last week for Moscow. We both agree that it is becoming difficult for us to travel. The worst is the journey to and from Sevastopol. The winding road makes us sick. The boat is no better. The sea is often choppy and incredibly smelly. The arthritis in her hands, particularly the right, has worsened to such an extent that she finds it difficult to hold a pen for more than a minute. "Writing letters is an ordeal, dear Masha," she has warned me. "If you don't get letters from me, this is not because I don't want to write and have stopped thinking about you, but because my hands are not up to it." We have decided to rely on the phone and to talk to each other as often as possible. A few words spoken and heard are far more reassuring than letters. But on the phone I have to be careful to keep my voice under control. Olga notices the slightest hesitation and the words "are you all right?" are enough to make me want to cry; and when I begin to cry, she too loses control. All the *prosti*, *izvenii*, *nu ladno*, *dovol'no* fail to settle the nerves. "I'll come, Mashenka," she consoles me, "whenever you need me. Just let me know; a word would be enough." But we both know these are mere words. She is too ill to travel and I am too frail to go to her.

A week before she left we went to Primorskii Park to have a look at Anton sitting on the greyish pedestal of rock called diorite. It was opened last July, and this was my second visit. "I understand your misgivings," Olga replied when I told her that it felt odd to come here and sit next to Anton, quietly watched by people walking past. "You don't need to look after this Anton," she said, holding my hand. "You've done your bit. This bronze Anton will manage nicely without you."

We both agree that we don't like the statue: Anton sitting on a rock, the left leg over the right, and to keep the composition symmetrical, the right hand across the left, with both resting on his knee. There is a small notebook in his left hand and his eyes are fixed on the sea just a few hundred metres across the park.

On the day 'he' was unveiled we couldn't decide if Anton looked sad, happy or indifferent. Olga spotted a hint of a smile resting at the corner of his right upper lip. To me his eyes looked hazy and sick. "The bronze doesn't suit him," Olga remarked, "but white marble would have been pretentious." I told her that I would have preferred Anton in grey and brown sandstone etched with ripple marks. Wood might have been even better; Anton carved inside the trunk of a cedar, looking out, not the whole body but only the face. "You have gone mad, Masha," Olga scolded me. Yes, Olga is right. Like his Dr Astrov, Anton loved trees, and would have grieved for years for the cedar sacrificed to keep him alive.

Chekhovu is the word in gold letters on the pedestal. Why 'To Chekhov'? Why not just his name, followed by 1860-1904? I should have asked Olga to explain. She would have found a simple and appropriate answer. "Don't complicate things, dear Mashenka," she would have added with a chuckle. "Not at our age." But the word and its symbolism do make me uneasy because I fail fully to grasp the intention of the sculptor. Would it be too simple to assume that this bronze Anton sitting on a rocky pedestal is some sort of offering to the real Anton, a way of saying thank you? Perhaps the statue, the pedestal and the space around it, including the wonderful cedars standing tall behind him, mark a place for him. It's Anton's place, where people come to remember him, a place where they can leave things such as flowers, postcards, poems, shells, pebbles, driftwood, or even bracelets. Elena Fillipovna tells me that often the guards in the park find bits of strange jewellery near Anton's feet. Is this bronze Anton meant to mark out a special space? Perhaps it is. Because Anton made our lives worth living, we have decided that this small corner of a seaside park should belong to him. Every time we pass, look in his direction and pause for a few seconds, we think of him.

***

Her name is Olga Sorina. 'Not another Olga!' I thought when she introduced herself. She is tall, taller even than me, and very thin, with beautiful soft, lightly-tanned skin. Her eyes are a mixture of blue and green and her nose so sharp and well-formed that I suddenly felt like touching it. What an embarrassing thought, I reprimanded myself, but it lingered for a while after she left. It has taken me a few days to realise that she has a glow, warm, kind and precious, that remains with you for days. When I sat down to write to Anton's Olga about her, my heart went mad, pounding for a few minutes so loudly that I was scared it would bounce out like the tennis ball with which her son Egorushka plays.

Olga's reply from Moscow is funny. "You have fallen in love, Mashenka," she writes, "which isn't bad at all. We need a spark in our old age to rekindle the desire of days gone by."

Yes, I have fallen in love. Not with Olga Sorina—I'll call her Olga S to avoid confusion—but with the freshness she exudes. She is young and driven, and this intimidates me, but I am pleased that she has come, as a reminder to me perhaps that it's never too late to have dreams. Wasn't I just like her, many years ago? That I hesitate to answer means that I probably wasn't. I was, I think, even then a little too responsible, a little too cautious and restrained. Only once did I allow myself to dream, and look how badly that ended. I learned my lesson quickly and forgot the key to the door that would have let little Alice walk into Wonderland.

But Olga S, I suppose, is a mere excuse. The secret lies with Egorushka. The mere utterance of his name makes my heart tremble, which isn't very good at my age. But I am not the only one enchanted by the little boy. Neither Elena Fillipovna nor Vera Ivanovna can keep their eyes off him. Olga S, I guess, is used to him, although I have occasionally seen her, too, looking at him enthralled.

The boy is only four, with silky blond hair and large blue eyes. His mouth is of the right size, with fairly thick lips, and his nose is even more beautiful than his mother's. But the most charming thing about him is his laugh. He laughs freely, and it rings like little bells. My heart aches each time I remember him laugh.

I saw Olga S near the statue last year. I was with Olga and I think Olga S was too shy to intrude and interrupt our tête-à-tête. A letter arrived a few weeks later in which she asked if she could come and see me and the house. She had a few interesting ideas which she wanted to talk over with me. I liked her as soon as she walked into the house. There is something special in her, so rare in people these days. The War ended almost a decade ago and yet most of us still seem cowed and diminished. Olga S has suffered too; the blockade must have left deep scars but strangely she seems to have come through almost unscathed. Almost, because there are times when the smile suddenly disappears and even the bubbling laughter of Egorushka isn't enough to cheer her up. Luckily the gloom doesn't last long.

At first, like his mother, Egorushka used to call me Maria Pavlovna. But after spending a few days alone with us, as his mother had to go to Sevastopol for an urgent consultation, I have become his Babushka Masha. It does sound a little strange, but I've come to like it. Even Olga is pleased, and I am sure a little jealous as well, that, so late in my life, I've acquired a charming little grandson. Her last letter to me begins "Dear Babushka Masha". In the spirit of the game I also ended my reply with "Babushka Masha". We are being silly, I'm sure we are, but little Egorushka is such a bundle of joy that I have suddenly stopped acting my age.

"Who is that?" he asked me the other day. He was in Anton's study staring at the portrait.

"Anton Pavlovich I replied.

"*Dyadya* Anton," he said, and glanced in my direction. I couldn't hide my smile at the word 'Uncle' and wanted to correct it to '*Dedushka*', but I didn't. Dear Anton in the portrait is too young to be called Grandpa, although I know he would have been very pleased if anyone did.

Olga S and Egorushka come to the house in the mornings. It's a little early for me but I am getting used to it. While we two are busy with our work he runs around in the garden and in the house, looked after by either Elena Fillipovna or Vera Ivanovna. At first they tried to stop him running in the house, but have now given up. He is too lovely to be locked in a cage. Let him run, shout, laugh, cry. The house needs it. I need it. We all need it.

Olga S knows that I wanted to be a professional painter and that school-teaching was merely a diversion. She also knows that I had the good fortune to learn a few tricks from a master like Isaac Ilyich Levitan. I didn't have to tell her the story of his *Haystacks in the Moonlight*, which hangs in Anton's study. She had already heard it, and although I had seen her looking at the painting several times, I guessed from the expression on her face that she wasn't impressed by it. I too find it a bit sentimental, a touch too pretty and nostalgic. Anton was missing the lovely Russian landscape and dear Isaac Ilyich had obliged; it took him less than half an hour to paint it. The speed with which he worked was amazing, so fast and yet with ease and authority. I have heard Anton brag about his own art: that if necessary he could instantly write a story about something as small and ordinary as a matchbox. He surely could, but he used to struggle as well especially with plays and novellas. To be around him then was a torture. He would sulk and complain and, bored, we used to disappear leaving him alone locked up in his study.

Isaac Ilyich used to boast as well, especially when there were pretty girls and women around. He loved their company. For a Jew like him it wasn't always easy. But he liked coming to Melikhova and spending time with Anton. They were good friends, but then one day, out of the blue, he came to me and proposed. I didn't know what to say.

I think Olga S knows the whole sorry episode but doesn't want to upset me by asking questions. But why should I be upset? If I cried then, it was just for a few minutes; and not because I was hurt but only because I felt that I had hurt Isaac Ilyich. He was so kind and I didn't want to disappoint him. Fortunately he took the rejection well, thanked me for being gracious and left. I had gone to Anton seeking his advice about the proposal but he didn't say anything. His silence resolved the matter there and then.

Do I feel bad? I don't know. I would have then, but it doesn't matter now. The sacrifices I made were willing, and I don't begrudge my life or feel betrayed, because what I got in lieu was also very precious.

Olga S is a painter too, and not a bad one either. Perhaps that is why we have found such quick rapport. Her drawings and water-colours are more exciting than the oils, but I don't want to discourage her. There is nothing wrong with the oils. It's just that some of them are a bit too abstract for me, at times too schematic and conceptual. Call me old-fashioned if you want, but a painting without a story always appears to me flat and empty. Is this why I like her drawings and watercolours more? Yes indeed, but there are other reasons as well.

***

We have decided it would be easier for all of us if Olga S and Egorushka were to stay with us at the house. It would save time and Olga S would be able to work in peace and quiet. We, the three babushkas, although Vera is a little young to be called a babushka, will share the task of looking after Egorushka. A room in the annexe has been aired and cleaned for him and his mother to sleep in at night. During the day Olga S will work in the room next to Anton's study, which used to be our mother's bedroom. It's not very big, but we have removed the divan and made room for her table. I am worried that the room in the annexe is dark, damp and cold and not very suitable for Egorushka. Perhaps we should set Olga S up in the corner of the dining room and let her and Egorushka sleep in the bedroom. We'll wait and see. We'll do our best that Egorushka spends most of his time outside: on the terrace and in the garden.

The weather this autumn is warm and the winds have suddenly disappeared. Anya, Elena Fillipovna's ten-year-old grand-daughter has agreed to come and play with Egorushka. I have tried to leave Olga S alone to work on her own; I only go and check if she is all right once or twice during the day. We often meet for tea and discuss her project.

The other day she asked me if I had any photos of Anton. I showed her the family portrait taken in 1874; I was eleven and Anton fourteen, I told her. She glanced at the photo, and from her look I surmised that although she liked it she had been expecting something different. The other picture of nineteen-year-old Anton didn't impress her either. I find Anton rather elegant in that: clean white shirt, black jacket and necktie. He always knew how to dress well, not to show off, but just to look decent. Showing off wasn't in his nature, although he could have if he'd wanted to.

Did he ever tell Olga about our miserable childhood in Taganrog? I don't think so. Even I wouldn't have dared tell anyone. To ignore it was much easier. But I am more than ever certain that Anton never forgot those awful years, and if he put so much value on decency and honesty in his later life, it was only because he had seen such ugliness so early. If I feel proud that I have lived honestly without ever betraying others or myself, the credit for that should go to dear Anton. He was my beacon, my support, my inspiration. Without him I would certainly have lost my way.

I asked Olga S if she was interested in the Taganrog photos of Anton. "Yes, please, Maria Pavlovna," she replied, unable to conceal her excitement. It took us a day to retrieve the box we needed. Because of the damage from water leaking in a few years ago, we had to put a lot of material away.

The packet I found had twelve photos. On the back of each was a date scribbled, most probably by me. I looked at my handwriting and realised how unsteady my hand has grown in the last few years. Lately I have tried as much as possible to avoid writing. Vera doesn't mind taking dictation. "It's nothing but bad spectacles," she tries to reassure me, but I know that my hands shake as soon as I decide to do something serious. And the problem isn't only with my hands; it's my mind, I am sure, that is going mushy. It just suddenly decides to wander without clear aim or intention. A blankness descends, and I am lost. Olga asks me not to worry about it because worrying exacerbates the situation. "We aren't young anymore," she repeats a thousand times, and to be honest, I find her nagging very irritating. Yes, irritable I have definitely become, and why shouldn't I be? It hurts to discover that you have lost control over your wretched body and mind. The body I don't care much about, but I do hope to remain lucid until the last day of my life.

Olga S saw the photos and her face lit up. She went to her table and brought back a big folder of her sketches. I glanced at them and immediately understood her eagerness to look at the childhood photos of dear Anton. Apart from a few very nice water-colours, most of her sketches were in black ink. "*The Steppe* is my favourite story," she said, "and these are my illustrations." The central figure in all of them was Egorushka; no, not her own Egorushka but the one in Anton's story. Is this why she named her son Egorushka? Most certainly, I hastily decided. Anton would have dearly loved this gesture, this kind tribute. But I was wrong. Egor is also the name of her late husband, Egorushka's father, who died a year after the child was born. "Of wartime injuries," Olga S explained.

In one of the drawings Egorushka is sitting in the back of a cart, the canvas roof of which has been removed; his arms are clasped round his knees, the cap has slipped off his little head, and his eyes are shut; he appears exhausted. In the second drawing he is looking in the direction of Khristofor, the priest; the old man with his thick beard, tinged here and there with grey, is ready to say his early morning prayers. The expression on Egorushka's face is a mixture of awe and bewilderment. One of the water-colours shows a night scene. It's called *The Steppe at Night*. The sky is dark and sprinkled with stars and Egorushka is lying in the cart on his back and looking up. He appears calm and (I don't know why) a little sad. Perhaps he is missing his mother; perhaps he is tired and sleepy, or perhaps it's the night itself. True beauty, dear Isaac Ilyich used to say, should always make you happy and sad at the same time: happy that it has come your way and sad because it won't last.

"He looks like Anton," I whispered, looking at the young boy in her sketches.

"He does," she replied.

"But not exactly."

"Just a little bit."

"And he does resemble your Egorushka."

"Yes, he does, because that's what I had first decided to do ..."

"But then realised that the Egorushka in *The Steppe* is in fact Anton," I couldn't stop myself interjecting. "Yes, that's right; there was always something child-like in the way Anton looked at the world. Both fascinated by its beauty and repulsed by its falsehood, but in the end the child always won. The wonder, the curiosity, the innocence never died."

"Yes, you are right, Maria Pavlovna. I had also suspected that, but wasn't sure. Now that you have confirmed it, I feel more confident. When I did these sketches in Leningrad I was merely guessing. I love the photos. They're wonderful. They'll help me to finish the sketches. I was waiting for a glimpse of his little face, just a mere hint and nothing more. The imagination should do the rest. Isn't that so, Maria Pavlovna?"

"Yes my dear Olga," I wanted to say. "Imagination is the key. To weave its beautiful magic it needs only a tiny window to look in or out. Too much reality can become a burden in itself."

Olga S wants to arrange an exhibition of her sketches and I agree that the Yalta house would be the most appropriate venue. One can do many interesting things with the sketches. They can be published as a book or printed separately as a series of picture postcards. The idea excites me and I am confident that the Lenin Library in Moscow will grant its approval and extend some financial support. I should write to Olga about the project. She can pull some strings in Moscow and muster resources. Yes, I should write to her immediately, or better, talk to her. She would love to see the sketches. I need to find out from Elena Fillipovna if we can send them to Moscow. I don't trust the mail, and Olga S agrees that it would be safer to find a reliable courier.

***

We have decided to go to Olga's dacha in Gurzuf. Olga S has left Egorushka with me. A letter from her husband's friend arrived last week, and she has gone to see him. He is a photographer who is arranging an exhibition of his wartime photos in Sevastopol. I myself wouldn't have left Egorushka behind, but I understand her misgivings about the journey. I have assured her that her son will be fine with us and that a week's separation won't be too hard for him to bear.

The weather is glorious and I believe that the sun, the water and swimming here will be very good for Egorushka. "He can't swim," Olga S warned. "We'll teach him," I replied without thinking. I should have been more circumspect. I am too old to teach him. Why do I get carried away so easily? If something untoward were to happen to him, Olga S, I suspect, would survive, but I would definitely die, of grief, no doubt, but of guilt and shame too. Anya is a good swimmer, and although she is just twelve she will keep an eye on Egorushka. Elena Fillipovna is also far more alert than I am; the two together will keep him away from danger.

Egorushka likes water. He has asked me many times to come to the creek with him to play. He doesn't realise that I am too old, and that if I slip and break a bone, it will be all over for me. He loves hunting for tadpoles and frogs and rushes to show them to me, stretching his little palm out, smiling, as if he has found the most valuable of treasures. "Ba…bush…ka Maa…shaa," he shouts, scaring the birds away.

On the beach he'll have sand and shells to play with and lots of gulls to chase. I had first thought of going to my own dacha in Miskhor, but Gurzuf is much safer because the bay is mostly calm and the water is not far from the hut, just a couple of minutes' walk. Moreover, the beach has sand, while the one at Miskhor is all pebble and none too pleasant to sit on. I talked to Olga in Moscow and she is pleased for us to stay at Gurzuf. "Have fun, dear Babushka Masha," she teases me. "Enjoy your grandson's company and don't forget to send me some photos of you together."

I know she is jealous, as I myself used to be when hearing her rave about her beloved nephew Lev and his son Andrei. It would hurt me to see how much she loved the little boy. During the War she spent most of her time worrying, trying to find a way to send money and food to Andrei and his poor mother, who had been evacuated to Tashkent. She was very annoyed with Lev for neglecting his wife and young son. I don't know if she has forgiven him even now. But enough about them. It isn't easy to forget the War, although for me it wasn't too bad. I would most probably have left Yalta, but to arrange transport became impossible, so I decided to stay behind to look after the house hoping that the Germans would leave us in peace. It's a miracle that both of us have come through the ordeal unharmed.

Now I know how risky it would have been to escape. The Germans didn't want anyone to leave: those who tried paid a heavy price. The steamer *Armenia* carrying escapees was bombed and they drowned. Most of us in Yalta saw it go down. It was horrible to see so many die. For days afterwards people on the beach gathered corpses, frozen, bloated, half-eaten.

***

We have returned from Gurzuf after spending three wonderful days on the beach. It's quite late in the evening and I am tired and want to go to bed, but Egorushka won't let me. He fancies running around the house demanding to be chased by Anya and me. I soon give up. Anya laughs when I try to convince him that he should leave me alone, and then whisks him away, carrying him on her back. They slip and tumble, laugh and scream, and I scold myself for being so mean. Yes, I miss peace and quiet in the house; yes, I want him to settle down, but I also fear that once he is in bed he will start asking for his mother.

Olga S will be back on Monday but will perhaps phone today or tomorrow. I don't know what effect that will have on Egorushka; I hope hearing his mama on the line doesn't distress him unnecessarily. He is so little, so vulnerable. I wonder how she is doing without him. "The first time is always difficult," I told her as she was leaving. This was a silly thing for me to say. It is never going to be easy, and the idea that with time we get used to partings and separations is a pure lie. Each time we leave behind the people we love, a bit of us dies. The anguish we experience is always fresh, unique and unbearable. That's what love does to you.

The three days on the beach were marvellous. If the weather hadn't turned bad we would have stayed in Gurzuf for a few more days. On Friday it started raining heavily and I was afraid that rocks from the cliff behind the hut would slide down and land on us. The wind blew hard, churning the water, which was unusually cold. I didn't have the patience to sit inside the hut and wait for the weather to improve.

I could see how disappointed Egorushka was. He adores the sea and the waves and wants to run into them continually. Not a trace of fear. Not a hint of hesitation. Joy, pure and simple. Anya's older brother Vovka had pumped up the rubber tube of a car tyre for Egorushka, and taught him how to stay afloat with it around him. I had to keep watching him, scared that, excited by his adventure, he would let go and drown. Near the beach is a small rock pool with enough water for him to flap and float, but he wouldn't go there, preferring instead the waves and foam.

Anya was very good; she knew how worried I was and kept a close watch, never letting him out of her sight. She tells me that she is very proud of Egorushka because he is so brave, and that in no time he will be able to paddle and float without assistance. I smile at the seriousness with which she expresses her opinion. She is quite a determined girl herself. I like her and hope that Elena Fillipovna won't force her to change. The thoughtfulness she demonstrates at such a young age is amazing. I wish I had been like her when I was young. I suppose some credit must also go to her mother, but the girl needs more love, care and guidance to grow and bloom to her heart's content. Failure to realise your dreams can be so devastating. Here I go again. Hopes and dreams. Come on now, there is no need to torture yourself. You did whatever was expected of you; you kept your promise, and if on the way you had to suffer, so be it. I think I am tired, that's why my mind is leading me astray. The exertion of looking after Egorushka has exhausted me.

The first day-and-a-half was pretty bad. It was silly to bring him to the beach without his mother, I couldn't stop telling Elena Fillipovna. Her response was always the same: "*Uspakoites* Maria Pavlovna," "*Vam nelzya*, Maria Pavlovna." "He will be fine," she repeated non-stop. She wanted me to lie down and enjoy the sun and let her and Anya look after Egorushka.

By the end of the second day I had relaxed. The sun was truly glorious, warm and friendly; the sea was benevolent, happy to sing sweet lullabies, and I slept so often that it became embarrassing. Even Egorushka didn't fail to notice my snoring. He would imitate the ungainly noises I made, and giggle. "Don't be so naughty," Anya would reprimand him, and take him away to play in the sand. Yes, watching him build castles was far less tiresome. I have noticed that he possesses a keen eye for shapes and colours; the pebbles and shells he gathered were quite special. That comes from his mother, I told myself, and the thought made me happy. Why? I don't know. I can't imagine myself as a mother. Would I have made a good mother? "Good, yes," I hear Olga's voice say, "but strict and miserly with affection." She is wrong. How would she know? Perhaps I should stop watching our little moon of a boy so closely. But how can I? He is so marvellous and *Slava Bogu* I have come to meet him.

"Slow down," I would want to tell him during the day, "the sea is not going to run away, and the sand will always be there for you." But he is driven, excited by the world keen to reveal itself to him. Then one day I found the most intriguing thing about him. He would be looking at the shells, picking them up and discarding them at will: the impatience with which he did this alarmed me. But suddenly he would find the shell he liked, and his whole demeanour altered. He would become full of concentration and intent, which I found even more alarming. These spells of intense concentration should exhaust him, I would think to myself, and when in the evenings I saw his lovely head slumped on the table half-way through his meal, I knew that I was right. I too would hurry to finish my meal and ask Anya to carry him to my bed. At night he snuggled up to me like a puppy and slept with his right arm folded tight around me. On the first night I wasn't able to get much sleep myself, worried that I might crush him. He would snore, mumble and moan, and that too would keep me awake.

On other nights he would want me to sing or tell stories. I had to explain that for an old woman of my age it wasn't very easy to sing.

"How old are you, Babushka Masha?" he would ask.

"Almost ninety."

"Is that a lot?"

"Yes, quite a lot."

"Are you going to die, then?"

"Yes, but not today or tomorrow. In a couple of years perhaps."

"That's all right then," he would say, give me a kiss and go to sleep.

I don't know why I have allowed myself to get so attached to this dear little boy. Olga would surely reprimand me for letting the situation get out of hand. "Dear Mashenka," she would pontificate, "the pleasure at our age turns into pain so quickly, that it's prudent to keep it strictly rationed." She is probably right, but I suspect she doesn't remember that something similar happens to the pain as well; like pleasure it too doesn't last long, and they both come from the smallest things imaginable. Their presence is transient and their transformation most regular. When one is young or perhaps not as old as I am now, pain in particular seems to last forever, gnawing like an angry squirrel at your heart, never allowing you that ultimate moment of grace when you are ready to say that you have forgotten the pain and the perpetrator too has been forgiven.

But I don't think I should blame Lydia Avilova for the distress she has caused. She wrote her letter because she felt the need; she was, I suppose, lonely and sad. And if through her letter she reminded me of the betrayal, it wasn't her fault at all, because the one who had betrayed my trust then was none other than my dearest Antonushka. Why this sudden turn of phrase, this awkward gesture of endearment? I have never ever called him Antonushka before. Anton was my older brother, my mentor, my mighty oak. Why is it that my heart trembles every time I look for a reason to blame him? The decision was mine, and if he chose to keep quiet it was only because he didn't want to interfere. To fault him in any way now would be unjust. He is gone and can't speak for himself. So let there be peace, and let silence be my sole companion.

But what about the letter? Its arrival was unexpected and its contents most sorrowful. The handwriting on the envelope seemed familiar; perhaps that's why I didn't open it immediately. The fact that I read it on the day the German Army invaded Poland was mere coincidence.

"A few years ago," wrote Lydia Avilova, "I was invited to spend the summer in a small village near Poltava. There I became acquainted with Aleksandr Ivanovich Smagin. It was a chance encounter but it soon turned into an enduring friendship. He was kind and incredibly honest and decent. I grew very fond of him, mostly because he would talk so lovingly about dear Anton Pavlovich, and, yes, about you. I don't quite know why, during one of our many lengthy conversations, he suddenly confessed his deep love for you. 'I haven't loved anyone else in my whole life,' he said. 'I love her even now,' he added after a pause. I can't forget the look on his face, sad but luminous. Now he is dead. I got the sorrowful news a few months ago. Please, Maria Pavlovna, do spare him a moment and remember his love for you. Let this, the remembrance, be his single great reward, and please don't be angry at me for reminding you about him. Yes, please don't be annoyed. I am old, weak and very sick, and expect to die soon. God only knows how much I crave to hear a kind word from you. As you know, like Smagin, I too have loved one and only one person in my whole life."

Yes, Anton did love her once upon a time. She was very lovable and he must have found something special in her; he was smitten. "Do you remember our first meeting?" he wrote to her. "It felt as if we had met before, and had found each other once again after a long separation."

At that time I wasn't sure about his feelings for her. It was an affair, destined to fail like so many others before and after: a *syuzhet* for a short story, he would have called it. I have never been able to make sense of his endless affairs. Towards women he was often very decent and honest, but there were times when he would remind me of Trigorin in *The Seagull*. So heartless and deceitful. But the women were equally bad, ready to pounce and conquer him. It was hard to keep them away from him; the worst thing of all was the deceit with which they used to compete with one another. Pathetic, they were. We used to call them 'Antonovkas' and laugh at them. His marriage to Olga didn't deter them either, making her whinge and whine. Over the years some became bitter and twisted, but there were many who still remembered him with love and affection. I think Lydia was one of the kinder ones, remaining loyal to him, unable to forget the brief moments of love and friendship.

I met Lydia a year later in Moscow. The trip was forced on me. Some urgent matters about the Yalta house had to be discussed with the authorities. I found Lydia living in a tiny room, damp, dark and oppressive. We sat round a small table littered with cigarette butts. She talked slowly, desperate to order her thoughts. The words resisted coming out; she paused to catch her breath, coughed a lot, and throughout our short conversation sipped coffee that smelled of vodka. I felt terrible, but it wasn't possible to help her in any way. I had my own problems to sort out. Our conversation was about trivial things, both of us taking care to avoid any mention of dear Anton or Sasha Smagin. As I got ready to leave she opened her little handbag and showed me a photo, the last one of Sasha Smagin.

He was a lovely man, tall and handsome, with the nicest of smiles, almost too eager to help in any way possible. It was very kind of him to travel with me to inspect properties near Poltava. Anton loved the rural lifestyle and he was keen to find a suitable house for us. We looked at several and a few were quite nice, but somehow it didn't work out. His proposal didn't surprise me and it took me only a couple of days to resolve the issue. 'Yes,' I would say, and get ready for marriage.

"You know, Antosha, I have decided to get married," I told Anton one day. He knew what was going on, and I had reason to believe that he was quite fond of Sasha Smagin. But he didn't say anything, leaving me to interpret his silence, which wasn't very hard. The matter was resolved easily. I surrendered once again; perhaps that is why it hurt so much to read his letter to Suvorin. "My sister," he wrote, "has decided against marriage, but the affair appears to continue through letters. The situation is beyond comprehension. The rumour is that she has declined the proposal once again."

Yes, 'once again'; but unfortunately we would enact the same scene a few more times and each time it would end the same way. The sad thing is that the embarrassment and pain I felt each time remained undiminished. I should have learned my lesson the first time and reconciled myself. Was I stupid, naïve or just confused? But he wasn't any help either. The silence he chose as a response was ambiguous and often irksome. Would I have accepted the proposal if he had given his approval? I don't know. I'm not sure at all. Did Anton ever feel guilty that because of him I repeatedly declined? He must have. But there was something odd with me as well. Was I too playing games with him, trying to win him over with my sacrifices? Was this a ploy to lay claim to him and his heritage? Heritage. What an awful word!

"Ba…bush…ka," I hear Egorushka calling. He is standing in the garden and wants me to come on to the balcony to look at something Anya has brought for him. "Look at my kite, Babushka Masha," I hear him shout. I walk out to the balcony, take off my reading glasses and look. It's a wonderful Chinese dragon-kite. Here they come now running up the stairs. Why can't they just walk? Why such a mad rush? Now they are on the balcony, full of excitement, and in no time the kite is set free; it sails above, etching strange wavy figures. They should be careful. There are so many tall trees around. If the wind falls and the kite comes down it will surely be trapped in the trees and we will have to ask Matvei, the old caretaker, to retrieve it. It wouldn't be easy for him. He isn't young either. Oh stop worrying, old hag! I hear myself saying. It's such a nice day; don't spoil it. Nothing can go wrong here. Look, Egorushka is holding the string. He seems so serious, trying hard to control the kite. When he gets tired he hands it over to Anya and gazes up in my direction. In his eyes there is nothing but joy. Don't let the shadow of the gloomy past come near, I tell myself. Don't let the moment decay. Keep it safe and alive forever, however short that forever might be.

***

Olga S has returned. She appears satisfied; the trip I think was fruitful. The exhibition of her husband's friend has opened, and the initial response isn't bad. She tells me that the photographer has given her some photos which may be of interest to me.

A strange thing happened when Egorushka saw her at the door, standing with her bag waiting for him. He didn't rush to her at once, but tried to hide behind my back. "Come on, my darling," his mother called.

"No," he whispered. "No, not at all."

"Why?" his mother implored, and then as she was about to turn he ran to her with such speed that I was scared he would slip and fall.

The two sat near the door, his head buried in her lap, sobbing. "It's all right, my dear," I heard his mother mumble. "No need to cry. I'm here now." And she smiled at me as if reassuring me that it was just a game, a sort of child's play. The scene lasted only a few minutes but I couldn't stop thinking about it for a long time. Egorushka had looked so happy and content in his mother's absence, enjoying, so it seemed, every moment he spent with us. Is he really that clever that he can hide his feelings so well? Does it mean that he was just pretending to be happy?

Elena Fillipovna was surprised that I took the whole thing so seriously. "With children, it's always like this," she tried to comfort me. "They're fickle as the autumn sunshine."

Three days have passed quietly. Nothing much has happened. Yesterday afternoon a small aeroplane flew quite low above the house, shaking all the windows and creating much excitement. It gave me a mighty scare. I still remember the German planes that flew over the house, low and threatening. Luckily the bombs then didn't hit the house itself, but most of the windows were damaged. It happened a day before the German Army left Yalta. Since that raid I haven't been able to look at the sky without fear. How strange that such fear doesn't ever completely leave you. Just when you feel that it has finally gone, it reappears with the same intensity.

Olga laughs at my confession and reminds me that she herself once flew in a small plane. It was a year or so before the War, at an air show near Moscow. She loved it, particularly the autumn forest as it unfolded beneath her, as if she were flying over a landscape painted by dear Isaac Ilyich.

Olga was intrigued that Olga S wanted to do my portrait. I was intrigued as well. The first time she asked me to sit for her, I didn't know what to say. 'What nonsense!' I blurted without thinking. She was startled by my response and I suddenly felt guilty. She didn't ask me again, but I felt she was waiting for me to change my mind. After a few days I started dropping hints that during the day

Anton's study had got the best light; that the balcony wasn't so bad either; and that my favourite place in the garden was the Gorkii Bench.

She doesn't want to do an oil painting and I agree with her. Black ink and water colours are much better. I love aquarelles. Their simple earthy look. An hour a day is enough for her. I am relieved too, scared that sitting longer might tire me and I might doze off.

Naturally we talk during the sittings. Egorushka doesn't disturb us. He keeps himself busy moulding strange animals from the wet clay Anya brings for him from the little creek in the garden. I ask Olga S to get some real clay for him, so that he can feel its soft oily touch, its earthy smell. Perhaps there is a sculptor hiding in him. She laughs. "He's just playing, Maria Pavlovna," and then after a pause adds that he wants to be a pilot, like his papa.

After one of these sessions, Olga S shows me a few photos she has brought from her husband's friend. Nikolai is his name. I look at them and quickly want to look away. They are horrible.

"It's a Nazi concentration camp," prompts Olga S.

"I know—I've heard about them. Olga told me last time she was here."

"This one is in Poland: Treblinka."

"I've heard about it. Wasn't it built to look like a normal railway station?"

"It was," she replies, and shows me another photo which makes me terribly sick.

In the photo I see an opened mass grave, and not far from it a dark grey mound, which Olga S explains is human ash. She tells me that it took eight to ten minutes for the male prisoners to undress and walk down to the gas chambers. The women needed five minutes more, because they had to have their hair shaved off.

I couldn't sit on the bench any more. I wanted to run away and hide, but as I got up to move, I lost control and slipped. Olga S saved me from falling down. But my spectacles came off and fell to the ground. The right-hand glass cracked.

I didn't speak to her for two days. Even little Egorushka understood that I was angry and left me alone. I wrote a short note to Olga S and asked Vera Ivanovna to deliver it. To keep these photos was dangerous, I said. They should be put away or destroyed. We need to wait for the right time, I cautioned her, to discuss such things openly.

She read the note and came out with a cup of tea for me, sat silently for a few minutes, and then apologised again. I tried to explain that it wasn't entirely her fault that I had become ill, but that she should have warned me before showing me the photos. I could see that she was really sorry, but looking at her I immediately realised that there was also something else bothering her.

"I am really sorry, Maria Pavlovna," she began, "but can I talk to you about something else?"

"What else? About the photos?"

"No, not about the photos, but…"

She waited for my response, and concluding that silence was a hesitant "yes", she asked: "Do you remember Dunya Efros?"

"Of course. She was one of my best friends. We had our differences but she always remained a friend."

"When did you last see her?"

"Many years ago. The last thing I received from her was a telegram from Germany. She had just read the news of Anton's death in a newspaper."

Then she asked me about the brief engagement of Anton and Dunya. "It was 1886," I told her. "Anton was twenty-six and Dunya a year younger. She wasn't very pretty, but she had presence and was charming in her own way. She was a bit shorter than me, quite shapely, with large expressive eyes and soft tanned skin. She had a largeish nose, but nowhere as big as the heroine's in Anton's *Tina*. I hate that story. Why did Anton choose to ridicule her openly? He shouldn't have. But Anton was Anton, a ruthless scavenger. Many of his friends turned against him after finding themselves in his stories. Some, like Dunya, were gracious enough to forgive his indiscretions, but for others it became a life-long offence against them. Dunya was definitely kind, but she was too temperamental for Anton, and too independent, too proud of herself, of her Jewishness. Often I would ask her to be more discreet, less daring but she would refuse to heed. She didn't want to convert, she had told me many times, but I suspect this wasn't the reason the engagement with Anton was called off.'

"Anton was very popular with women, a sort of Don Juan. The friends he had in those days were a bit loose as well. They would drag him around to unsavoury places. Dunya was quite aware of that, and I suppose that's what must have forced her to change her mind. She must have felt insecure with so many women vying for Anton's attention. He wasn't ready to start a family then. We all depended on him, financially and otherwise. Without him, we were doomed. Perhaps he wanted to leave us, to start a family of his own and escape. What a horrible idea! No, I can't be right. Anton wasn't like that at all. He would have soon realised that with a new wife it would be difficult to keep on helping us. Perhaps that's why he broke off the engagement, or perhaps it was Dunya who didn't want to go ahead with the marriage. She was quite determined, you know."

"And then she married a lawyer from Taganrog?"

"Yes——Efim Konovitser was his name. The times were bad. The police were expelling the Jews from Moscow. She decided to leave, go south, at least for a few years. But we remained friends and she and her husband came to visit us in Melikhova a few times."

"And then she went to France …"

"That was after the October Revolution. She had always wanted to go there. One of Olga's actor friends probably met her in Paris just before the War. I'm not sure. So many Russians left to live an unsettled life in Germany or France, unable to make any sense of the world in turmoil. Dear Ivan Bunin, he used to stay in the bedroom you two sleep in now; he also emigrated. He sent me a postcard from Germany. He passed away in Paris in November last year, a heart attack, they say. In a way it's good that he didn't return to Russia. Sasha Kuprin too should have remained abroad. Returning ruined him completely. He knew it would, but he couldn't stop himself; he wanted to be laid to rest here. Silly he was, utterly idiotic. Dunya must be quite old now, a few years older than me. A happy grandma, I suppose …"

As soon as I said these words, I realised that there was something wrong. The words somehow didn't feel right. Yes, words are only words, but often they give away the lie they are supposed to mask. The voice betrays us. It betrayed me too and, as I looked up, the expression on her face confirmed it. "She was eighty-two, perhaps a few months older," Olga S said, "when she must have walked naked, her head shaved, up the path to the gas chambers of Treblinka …"

"O *Bozhe*!" I wanted to say, but soon realised that there was no place for God in this conversation. None whatsoever. If there was no God for Dunya at that railway station, how can I let Him near us now?

There was nothing else to say after that. I decided that silence would be my abode, my escape, my way to cope with the dreadful news.

I didn't speak to anyone for many days. Then at last I decided to phone Olga. I told her about the fate of Dunya Efros, and the two of us cried and cried. "Don't cry, dear Mashenka," she said, but her words made me sob even more. She said that if I wanted she could catch the next train and come to Yalta, to give me a big hug and to visit Anton in the park. "We'll go to him, dear Masha," she said, "and sit with him and tell him the story of Dunya Efros."

I declined her offer. She is too frail to make such a long journey. I had phoned her because she alone would feel my grief. I just wanted to cry with her, like old women of my age do. Nothing more.

***

No pain is endless and no grief inconsolable. How could it be otherwise? A distraction is all that we need. But the sudden illness of Egorushka wasn't the distraction I was looking for.

A day after my conversation with Olga in Moscow, little Egorushka fell ill. At first we thought that it was just a mild cold with a little cough and some congestion that would soon pass. But it didn't. His cough worsened and within two days his temperature rose.

"Maria Pavlovna!" I heard a frantic knock at my door. It was past midnight. "It's me," I heard Olga S call. Then she pushed open the unlocked door and rushed in, desperate, almost mad. "He is dying, Maria Pavlovna—really!" she wailed.

Luckily I had already asked them to move to the bedroom next to Anton's study. That's where I found the poor little boy, feebly breathing. His body was burning hot. We took his temperature. Forty degrees Celsius.

What to do? I was clueless. "We have to bring his temperature down. Immediately," I heard her plead. There was a tub full of water downstairs. His mother carried him down. We stripped his little lamb of a body naked, and lowered him into the cold water. His body convulsed—once, twice, and then his eyes opened for a second. We let him lie there for a few minutes. His body stopped shivering. Only a gentle bird-like flutter occasionally ran through it.

We took him gently out of the tub and carried him to the bedroom. I asked his mother to run down to the annexe, wake up Matvei and send him for Yuri Nikolaevich, the doctor, who fortunately lived just across the street. Before he came, we took Egorushka's temperature again. It was still high, but had gone down by two degrees. His breathing was more regular and he started moaning.

Yuri Nikolaevich came at once. He examined him, listened to his breathing, took his pulse and said that he would have to go to hospital in the morning. He told us that giving the little boy a cold bath wasn't a bad idea, and it was good that his temperature had fallen. He asked us to give Egorushka aspirins to keep the temperature low. He said that Egorushka had a severe infection of the right lung and that he sincerely hoped it had not advanced to pneumonia. He showed us how to use icepacks to cool down his body, and told us to keep an eye on his coughing.

Egorushka spent ten days in the hospital. He has come back to the house now, but is still too weak to walk. During the day we bring his bed out to the balcony. The days are sunny and warm. From the balcony we can glimpse a little bit of sea. Occasionally a steamboat or ship blows its horn, and Egorushka's eyes light up. He hasn't forgotten the trip to the Gurzuf dacha, and wants to go there again. His mother has promised him a trip to Sevastopol to show him the huge naval ships with their big guns.

Olga S looks so exhausted that I'm scared she might fall ill herself. "I have work to finish," she reminds me every time I ask her to relax. She is convinced that by spending a month with us in the house she has made herself a burden, and that the time has come for her to pack and return to Leningrad. "It will be cold and windy there," I intervene, but she ignores my advice. Slowly I am beginning to understand her decision. She needs to get back to her job in the city where some interesting commissions are awaiting her. She tells me that next summer she will try and come to Yalta again, to finish work on the sketches for her exhibition.

When I ask her about Egorushka, she smiles and assures me that she would never come without him, and that if I am not busy at the time, she would like him to stay once more in the house. She reminds me that Egorushka hasn't forgotten his Babushka Masha, and his swimming lessons with the pumped-up tube. She promises that she will arrange swimming lessons for him and that by next summer he will be ready to swim on his own.

They're going then, I tell myself, and begin to think about all the things I have neglected since their arrival. I too need to return to my daily routine. It can't go on like this for much longer. I have the house to look after, and it needs more money for urgent repairs. But I am tired of begging.

Anya has bought a new kite for Egorushka. He is still pale but the smile has come back. "You can fly it in Leningrad," she tells him.

"I will," he replies, "and ask mama to send you a photo with the kite."

***

A week has gone by with no word from Leningrad. I suppose Olga S and Egorushka have more important things to worry about.

I have packed away the toys Egorushka forgot to take with him. A few lumps of dried clay he moulded, painted by Anya, sit on my desk, but all other signs of their presence in the house have been removed. This helps me get back to my normal everyday life.

To be honest, I don't manage the day-to-day running of the Museum these days. Everything is in the hands of Elena Fillipovna and Vera Ivanovna, although nothing happens without my consent. Whenever I feel like it, I browse through the archival material, photos, papers and other little things. Every time I sift through the packets and files I expect to be surprised, and more often than not I am. I know that most surprises are because of my failing memory, which has become more and more unreliable. In a way it's good that I've stopped remembering so many things. It's easy to keep going when the baggage you carry is small and not very important.

That I was looking for something became clear to me as soon as I found in a folder an old postcard from dear Ivan Bunin. Anton has a story, I can't recall its title, but the main character is a Portuguese painter, Don Zinzaga. Dear Ivan, I remember, had started calling himself Don Zinzaga and I became his Lady Amaranta. Sounds silly, but it was quite funny at the time. For many years we played this game. "Dear Amaranta", he would begin his letters, ending them with "Your humble slave, Don Zinzaga". Did I write him letters in a similar vein? I suppose I did. I must have, knowing that nothing serious would ever come of this game.

Now I understand why he decided to take refuge in France. He was very French in style and taste, although his soul was nothing but Russian. Anton, perceptive as he was, coined a special name for him: 'Monseigneur Bukishon from France'. How did he endure his life there? I heard that he wasn't happy and took to drink.

The postcard has a German stamp. "I am in Berlin," the short note begins, "dear and much respected Maria Pavlovna, travelling for weeks in Germany. Three years ago I was passing through Berlin on my way to Stockholm to collect the little prize they had bestowed on me. I have mixed feelings about it; I am proud that I have won it, and it came with money I definitely needed, and need even more now, but that I am the first Russian belletrist to receive it saddened me. Lev Nikolaevich deserved it more than anyone else, and dear Anton Pavlovich should have been next on the list. I was embarrassed, and perhaps that's why I didn't write. But I write to you now because I see dark clouds hovering over Europe. The possibility of catastrophic war has become quite real. What's going to happen to us all? Please do take care of yourself, dear Maria Pavlovna, and may God keep you safe and out of reach of the misery that is going to fall on us soon."

The next letter in the file seems to have arrived five years after the War. It was sent from Grasse, which my atlas tells me is somewhere in southern France, a nice coastal town with warm summers. There was nothing special about the letter except a few lines about his short book of memoirs about Yalta and Anton. He wanted me to look at his manuscript and see if it was all right. I don't remember if I sent a reply. I must have, but I certainly don't recall sending back the manuscript. I should ask Vera Ivanovna; she would know.

The letter came with a postcard-size print of a painting, a small and rather dull reproduction of the original. I don't remember if Ivan ever liked Chagall. I didn't either, at least initially. Slowly, however, I started appreciating his strangely-proportioned figures often half-hanging above the ground, as if in ecstasy. But this painting is unusually melancholic. *Solitude* it's called. I like the cow with its big sad eye, a tear ready to drop. But what's that violin and bow doing there? In the background the city is covered in dark smoky clouds, and in the blue cloudless patch a white angel is flying off, as if abandoning it. To the left of the cow a sad-looking man, a Jew in a white tallith, is sitting on green grass holding in his right hand the red scrolls of the unopened Torah. His inclined head rests on his right arm. The white tallith, the white cow and the white angel in the sky form a strange, sad triangle. I look at the face of Ahasverus, the Wandering Jew, and in this face see traces of Anton. I imagine pince-nez and the resemblance increases. Sasha Kuprin was right when he wrote that most people who met Anton wrongly thought that his eyes were blue. He had dark, almost black eyes, similar to the melancholic Jew's in the painting.

As I look at it I know that it's no coincidence that I'm staring at it now. These coincidences have their own hidden logic. I'm certain that if not the painting, something else would have fallen in front of me to remind me of the sad story.

Three weeks have gone by since I saw those terrible photos of Treblinka, and although I have tried my best to forget them, to save myself from unbearable pain, I know that I haven't stopped for a minute grieving for poor Dunya Efros. O Dunya, poor Dunya! I hope your children somehow managed to avoid the death camps. I hope someone helped them escape. I hope they are still alive.

Even if they are hurt, bruised, scarred, please let them still be alive. I hope they remember you and grieve for you. I hope they have named one of their daughters Dunya. I hope when they look at her they also think of you.

I am too old, my dear Dunya, to travel now. Otherwise I would have gone to Treblinka, shaved my hair and walked the path you once walked. I certainly would have done this, and I know that Anton would have too. But I also know that this would never be enough to make up for the pain you endured. It is easy to share joys and pleasures with others, but the pain we suffer is always our own, unique and endless. And yet we do our best to share whatever we can of the pain our loved ones have suffered, because pain endured in our own unique way confirms our humanity.

Perhaps I should write to Olga S to see if Nikolai the photographer, her late husband's friend, knows someone who can visit Treblinka for me. I would like them to go to the camp and light a candle. Anywhere along the path to the dreadful showers would be enough. Light a candle, even a tiny one would do, and sit with it until it burns down; gather a few drops of wax and post them to me. That's it. Nothing more.

But would the wax tears bring consolation? I really don't know. Perhaps they would. But do I want to be consoled and comforted? No, I want to suffer and grieve and carry the grief with me undiminished, until I die. Only death will bring me relief. Redemption I don't want to think about. I haven't sinned. My benevolent God, I'm sure, understands that, and the feeling of guilt which troubles my heart is also understood and condoned by Him. But my guilt isn't strictly mine. I am guilty by association, guilty that I have lived in times so unbelievably cruel and inhumane, and that I didn't have the courage to speak up. I should have. I definitely should have.

Like others, I too was selfish, too concerned to save my own skin.

But—

I hate the word. All excuses begin with this terrible word.

Tommaso Campanella

Tommaso Campanella (1568-1639)

Giovanni Domenico Campanella was an Italian philosopher, theologian, astrologer and poet. He was born in a village near Stilo, Calabria. His father was a poor and illiterate cobbler. He entered the Dominican Order when he was fifteen and adopted the name Tommaso in honour of Thomas Aquinas.

Campanella's heterodox views, particularly his opposition to the authority of Aristotle, brought him into conflict with the Inquisition. He was also involved in organising rebellion against the Spanish occupation of parts of Central and Southern Italy. Campanella spent close to thirty years in prisons, at times brutally tortured. He is known to have intervened in the first trial of Galileo Galilei and published a pamphlet *Apologia pro Galileo* in his defence. Between 1626 and 1634 he lived in Rome and for a few years enjoyed the patronage of the Pope Urban VIII. He published his most famous work *La Cita del Sole: Dialogo Poetico* (*The City of the Sun: A Poetical Dialogue*) in 1602 (revised in 1623).

The monologue is set in Rome. The year is 1633.

The world's a theatre: age after age
Soul masked and muffled in their freshly gear
Before the supreme audience appear,
As nature, God's own Art, appoints the stage.

Each plays the part that is his heritage;
From choir to choir they pass, from sphere to sphere,
And deck themselves with joy or sorry cheer,
As Fate the comic playwright fills the page.

[*Nel Teatro del Mondo*, Tommaso Campanella]

On this cold and rainy morning of *dies cinerum* I'll go to the basilica, walk up to the altar and Frate Antonio will dip his thumb in the blessed ashes, mark my forehead with a black smear and whisper: "remember that thou art dust and unto dust thou shalt return." Amen, I'll say to myself and walk away humbled.

That I should feel humbled is most appropriate because from tomorrow the fasting will start and I will partake in physical and spiritual purgatory. I will desist intake of food and limit myself to two little bowls of lukewarm milk, one each in the morning and evening, and resist all temptation to converse with anyone. I'll take the vow to be silent, my Lord: *That my mouth may not speak the words of men: for the sake of the words of thy lips …*

I'll repeat the words and walk up and down the long corridor, till my legs and feet are benumbed. I'll sit for a while in the corner and make myself disappear in the darkness listening to the hushed footsteps, the rustle of black habits, the murmuring of prayers, and remain silent. At night I won't sleep a wink more than four hours and I will wake up early, before anyone else has woken, and pray; and pray I must: *he shall be like a tree which is planted near the running waters, which shall bring forth its fruit, in due season. And his leaf shall not fall off …*

Did I also feel like a tree planted near the running waters? In some ways I did, otherwise how could I have survived for so long with my enemies waiting for me to stumble and then pounce on me to inflict a fatal blow. They haven't disappeared and the sorry stories of last year's trial have strengthened their resolve. Perhaps I should accept the invitation and abandon this city for Paris. The waters of the Seine they say are calm, less odorous, and more healthy than those of the murky Tiber.

***

Last night was the night of the *moccoli* and I am glad that I persuaded myself to go out for a walk—of my last, so my heart tells me, carnival. Thousands of twinkling tapers set the Corso aglow, mimicking the sky littered with stars of all sizes and hues. The Corso too ebbed and flowed like a stream in the Milky Way. I felt light and free and let myself float with the crowd, sailing in a celestial boat drifting gently towards the heavens. But the lightness was momentary and the exhilaration brief and ephemeral.

Ten days ago as the bell on the Capitoline rang announcing the beginning of the carnival I resolved that I would keep away from it, that I would even avoid the *moccoli* and stay confined to my cell and work patiently on the book. I have truly no interest in the masks, the confetti battles and the Barbary horses racing in the Corso; it is all too boisterous and frivolous. But then the day of the *moccoli* arrived and I couldn't resist the temptation. I went out and noticed that I didn't have a candle with me. Quite appropriate, I had told myself. To carry the faintest of lights this year would be shameful, a betrayal of the worst kind. I'll let darkness find a lasting abode in my heart and shun every sound of hope. My Lord understands the depth of my despair. If he has allowed despondency to subdue my will, only he will bring joy and redemption. The joy will come. No doubt it will. I just have to wait and be patient: *All things have their season, and in their times all things pass under heaven.*

This city, I am convinced, has a heart of darkness. The Romans know it better than me, although they never stop crowing that it sits at the very centre of the world; that divine light emanates from it in all directions delivering our Lord's grace and benevolence. During the day, even when cloudy and gloomy like yesterday, the city shines, but at nights it falls prey to the darkness so readily that like others I have often dreaded that the night would never pass.

At night the darkness rules the streets. The *lampioncini* before the Madonnas at the street corners never quite succeed to break its hold. I have failed to comprehend why the Romans find the street lights meretricious—*l'insidia dei lumni*, they often say. Darkness, they argue, provides cover, anonymity and freedom; *volti la luce*, turn the light away, a passer-by will often tell you on the street, anxious to remain unnoticed. To walk at night is quite perilous because the carriages drive without lamps and one needs to carry a small lantern to remain

76

visible, but often the carriages speed and fail to notice the hapless pedestrians. I too have suffered at the hands of these impatient fools; luckily each time I have escaped with minor bruises. The walk back afterwards without a light is even more perilous; you have to wait for someone with a lamp to emerge and follow him, hoping that his destination isn't so far from your own.

I am not a Roman and to be honest I don't have the slightest desire to become one. I remain stubbornly Calabrian, the uncouth peasant, who finds it rather arduous to harbour any fondness for the Romans. Not all Romans are cunning, vain and pretentious, I do concede, but the proximity to power has definitely corrupted many souls.

The grandeur of the city scares me and often I walk to the ancient ruins in search of peace. The ruins abound in the city and flocks of goats graze freely among them; the bulls lie in the shade of tall obelisks, and many courtyards, cris-crossed by the shadows of shattered columns, have been turned into henruns and cowhouses. My favourite place is the Forum, now the site of a large cattle market; the weeds grow everywhere and the walls of the ruins are buried under heaps of dirt and refuse. The arches near the Basilica of Constantine are surrounded by mounds of rubble and the space between the arches is walled and used as stables. The last time I went to see the Baths of Caracalla I found a young Spanish friar busily sketching the huge trees growing in the arches; in the crevices of the walls I saw strands of jasmine and acanthus and bushes of wild roses. I sat for a while on a marble seat that had escaped the attention of the invasive ivy, watching a flock of birds feeding happily on the blackberries growing over the stoneworks.

The ruins and the signs of steady encroachment of nature over man-made creations are strangely sobering. A calmness settles in me and I begin to recognise that although the world around me is going mad, the refuge from it, my Lord tells me, isn't very far. Keep looking for it and be ready for the moment when it announces itself. Sitting amongst the ruins my ears are quickly attuned to the sounds that nature of its own will and necessity makes; the natural rhythm touches invisible cords and someone inside me begins to sing. Is it my mother? I ask, and hear my father call, "Caterina". I wait for her to come out of the house but she doesn't; I only hear the shuffle of footsteps across the cold stony floor. Caterina, my mother, died when I was fighting my own death in the dungeon of Castel Saint Elmo. Mario, my cousin, who brought the news also brought the rusted iron cross she had worn since she was a child. I kissed it and put it around my neck and there it has remained since. It had her smell and touch and most strangely the sounds of the same whisper-like walk. She is with me all the time, I would often think and the thought would bring joy and relief. O how gullible the heart is, I would tell myself: so easy to please and comfort and so ready to be fooled. But there was magic in the sound of the name; Caterina, I would hear someone call on the street or in the market and a pleasant shiver would run through my body. I would look around to ascertain the source of the call and walk away unable to quell its bell-like toll.

Why did the bells sound so different in Napoli? Was it because of the sea and the salty wind or was it because of Vesuvius spewing its sulphurous emanations? I don't know, but I do miss the bells. Such beauty in a city so severe. Why did I want to go back, my good friend Signor Gabrile Naude had asked me once. To die, was my answer. He looked bemused and I had to explain that there was no irony in my reply, no falsehood of any kind, but truth, stark and bare, like the death I had come face to face with several times there. My God had willed me to endure the unendurable and endure I did. Yes, it was His will: *The Lord is my light and my salvation, whom shall I fear? The Lord is the protector of my life: of whom shall I be afraid?*

Seeing that my dear friend wasn't satisfied with the explanation I decided to tell him about Don Basilio Berllario. He was, I am sure, my Lord's special messenger—the true harbinger of hope and salvation. He was my enlightened adviser, my guide, my confessor. He saw that I was crippled with doubts and asked me to pray and I had prayed: *For though I should walk in the midst of the shadow of death, I will fear no evils, for thou art with me. Thy rod and thy staff, they have comforted me. Thou hast prepared a table before me against them that afflict me. Thou hast anointed my head with oil; and my chalice which inebriatheth me, how goodly is it . . .*

The doubts were dispelled and my soul touched by his hand healed; I had rediscovered the sense of my blissful being. But I haven't forgotten the inferno, and the memory of my safe passage through it is still alive. Thus to thank my wise steersman I want to go back; to pray for his kind soul I want to go back; to realise that I am frail and fallible, I want to go back.

The trials the Lord erects for us have a purpose, and the purpose is simple—to confirm that the threads which bind us to him aren't bare and that although it's sensible to remember our success in overcoming adversities, it's more prudent not to forget the ordeals themselves. Out of love for us does he send us pain and we should cherish the pain as much as the pleasure that results from the healing he brings about. He loves us and in love does he command us to find our humanity.

A few years ago I received a note from Signor Del Tufo, the keeper of the library in Castel Nuovo, informing me of the death of Don Berllario. He died from severe illness caused by an unyielding bout of sweating sickness. I hope there still exists a little space for me near his grave in the cemetery on the green slopes of the hill overlooking the bay and the salty air floating over the turbulent waters of the sea.

How can I forget the sea? Always furious and yet strangely soothing. To the sea I am grateful for keeping me sane and sensible; the incessant rumbling and splashing of waves made the oppressive silence bearable. During the storms the foamy water would sprinkle through the tiny hole of the window and wet my face, waking me up from sleep, often short and erratic. *I have carried the sea in my ears*—these are the words of my first sonnet. I owe them to the sea and to the mercy of our Lord. At night I would shut my eyes and let the sounds pour in, and in no time they would swell into sheets of water, flapping me around like driftwood. On such nights I would endeavour to keep myself awake hoping that they would turn into verses of exquisite beauty. In the morning I would begin to scribble them down, enthralled by their unworldly elegance; they have come straight from the lips of our Lord, I would tell myself and cherish every little sound and word. He is the source of all beauty. I would pray and ask him to remain gracious and loving and to drive away any semblance of hatred that had knowingly or unknowingly entered my heart. I am no Homer or Virgil but I do pray to our Lord to bless me with ears sensitive to the faintest of sounds the world so lovingly designed by Him makes.

***

My friends remark that I spend a considerable amount of time walking; even inside the convent I can't stop pacing up and down, they seem to complain. They must find the unrelenting noise of my steps irritating; occasionally it irritates me as well, but I am sure I don't have to tell them the reason. If my behaviour appears to them compulsive, they should think of the years that I have spent in cells so small that the thought of taking even ten paces inside at a time would have been a wishful dream. I walk because it helps me to drive away the oppressive thoughts, but often they don't readily ease their hold and I am forced to seek refuge in music which appears almost unasked—a lute or a cornetto, and floating above them a voice. But most of all I love the *Cuncti Simus Concanentes*—the basso voice accompanied by delicate flute and rhythmic beat of drums. The pace of my steps soon synchronises with the beat and if I am alone, my arms begin to move. I feel free and light—such bliss, but alas it occurs so rarely and lasts for such a very short time.

Last night as I walked in the direction of the Corso, I didn't need the music to ease my anxiety; I was excited—nothing too outrageous, just a mild tingling in the heart—waiting to experience the delights of the luminous night. However, slowly the mood changed; the spring in my steps disappeared, my pace dropped and I began to be troubled by unwieldy thoughts. But I didn't stop because I knew that the escape from them lay only in walking them out of my mind.

Just in front of Palazzo De'Carolis I saw two ladies in beautiful dresses and elaborate shawls catch fire; they were trying to save their candles from being extinguished by a rival pair. There was a great commotion but luckily the incident ended without injuries. I saw people walking with long poles and a damp rag attached at one end; these poles are used to blow out the candles of your rival. A young man had brought a set of kitchen bellows; his success was applauded but there were some who condemned the bellows as most inappropriate and unbecoming.

Normally I continue my walk along the Corso to reach the bottom of the Piazza del Popolo, the place from which the procession of lights begins. I like walking upstream, avoiding boisterous revellers and ignoring their frivolous and often caustic remarks. They must find the presence of a friar, large, ugly and severe, odd. Last night, however, I changed the route. I hadn't planned to but it happened quickly and without much thought. Near Chiesa Sant Marcello a fight broke out. An old man with a hatchet had attacked a young cavalieri walking alongside a pretty boy. The old man was drunk and missed the cavalieri and landed the blow on the boy who immediately collapsed with blood gushing from his right shoulder blade. The young cavalieri didn't help him, saw the blood and the old man, and scurried away. The crowd gathered around the two. The old man wept. Perhaps the boy was his son, I had thought, and turned back in the direction of Palazzo Venezia. At the palazzo I turned right and continued walking up Via San Marco. The streets here were quiet, untouched by the hustle bustle of the *moccolli*. I don't remember how but after some time I found myself in Campo dei Fiori.

Why Campo dei Fiori? Was it the moon looking hesitantly from behind the clouds leading me on? It must have been so because as soon as I stepped into the

Piazza, thick shafts of light from the sky fell on the cobblestones littered with animal shit and puddles of yellowish piss.

I thought about going to the ghetto to meet my dear friend Abram Levi. I would knock at his door, I had imagined, and he in spite of the late hour would open the door without delay and welcome me with a smile; I would smile in return and we would hug; his five-year old granddaughter would rush to greet me and climb over me, insisting to touch the seven nutty bumps on my hairless skull. Just once, Abram would warn her, and she would soon disappear inside the small house bustling with people, to leave us to converse in peace. He would show me the books he had recently received from Paris, London or Antwerp, telling me stories about them, their authors, illuminators and printers. I would complain about bad sleep and rheumatic pains and he would ask me to try his favourite potion made from a mixture of olive and almond oils, with a few drops of an extract from a root from far-away China. We would talk about this or that but steadfastly avoid any gossip about Signor Galilei, his trial and his hasty departure from Rome late last year, knowing well that we both hate the encumbrance we have unwillingly imposed upon ourselves.

I don't think I consciously avoid the dreadful Campo dei Fiori but it appears that the more I keep away from it the stronger its hold on my mind grows. Does this mean that I should let it have its way? Like a reed I should learn to bend where and when I have to bend, sway when I have to sway and let the water swirl and surge as much as it likes? Once it has come to know that giving in is my preferred mode of resistance, perhaps it will leave me alone. But will it ever leave me alone? I don't know, because there isn't anything more grievous in the world than fear. No, of death I don't fear at all; let it come whenever it decides to and I'll accept it with grace and humility; the merciful Lord has equipped me wisely to welcome it with open arms. If He wants me to live, live I will, and if He wishes me to abandon my mission, abandon I must. Like a loving father He continues to assay the strength of my love, and when faced with fear I lose faith in Him, He extends His hand to rescue me from oblivion. It is His will that guides me to this place and the purpose, I know well, is simple—to force me to confront my fears and to harden my resolve to overcome them. If I win, and win I surely must, the victory won't be mine. To Him will go all the credit and the glory too will be His, for He is the Lord and the Master.

In Campo dei Fiori I saw the tall gibbet in the middle of the piazza and stopped, amazed by its long moon-lit silhouette on the stones. Just a few steps to the right was the fountain, covered by a curved marble slab, and I decided to walk around it. On the little platform near the gibbet someone had put three candles, a bowl of water and two green apples. An old mare with watery eyes lay beside it. She looked at me, snorted angrily and turned her head away. The water in the fountain gurgled and as I stretched my hand to touch the cold marble covering the fountain a pigeon fluttered its wings and hopped away. Behind the gibbet, not far from the front entrance of the Cancellaria Apostolica a small crowd had gathered. They were drunk and abusive and wanted two women to sing and dance. One of them, a young girl of twelve or fourteen, looked terrified. A few steps away from them sat an old woman roasting chestnuts. She glanced in my direction and immediately turned her face away. I bought from her two small cups and asked her to take them to the young girl. As I was about to leave she asked me to wait for a few more minutes. A white stallion would appear in the sky, she told me, just after the crescent had emerged from behind the palazzo. The stallion would fly from left to right, she waved her hand, then right to left; the trumpets would sound and the stallion would descend, trot a circle round the gibbet and fly away.

The old woman wasn't mad. The stories about the white stallion landing in the Campo dei Fiori were well known and the association with Giordano, the unfortunate Nolan, quite obvious. He was brought to the stake stark naked, I had heard from Gaspar Scioppius, who had come to visit me in the cell. It was an hour after midday and the day was dull, cold and windy. Before he was tied to the pole his tongue was gagged to smother screams and blasphemies. For three long hours he had burnt, and they say the executioner who came to collect the ashes in the evening after the crowd had dispersed had found a dead white stallion near the gibbet. Francesco Pucci, the Navarrist, I had thought then, was somewhat fortunate. He was beheaded in the prison, a quick, instantaneous, and I hate to say, painless death, and the dead body burnt tied to the same gibbet.

If these thoughts make me miserable, so be it because the killing and the burning, I am convinced, will continue unabated. There is hardly a day in Rome when a man or a woman isn't sent to the galleys. Only a week ago two young men were hanged in the Piazza dei Santi Apostoli. They had been caught smuggling tobacco. A placard was hung on their backs announcing their crime and they were marched to the Piazza by the executioners dressed as *pulcinelli*; the crowd jeered and shouted insults and as heavy knives fell on them, it chanted in unison: "Think of your souls, you wretched creatures, and pray. Have mercy on them O

Lord and have mercy on us." How strange, I had thought. We kill in the name of justice, divine or otherwise, and then console our victims by praying for their doomed souls.

The woman took the chestnuts to the girl and that's when for no particular reason I decided to look up, and I am glad that I did, because the clouds had miraculously dispersed revealing a sky spluttered with stars: right overhead a prostate Leo and to its right my own Virgo, but it was the Ursa Major that stole the show. My eyes found the two stars at the end of the handle and they guided me to Arcuturus, the brightest of them all, and yellowish like a fresh lemon. I turned around searching for Spica, the pale white pearl. It was hidden behind a thin blob of a cloud and without waiting for it to move away I began to traverse my way to Virgo's diamond. It would have been nice to spread a blanket on the ground, lie down and let the stars guide me across, but soon I felt dizzy and decided to walk out of the piazza. I cast a final glance in the direction of the gibbet and hurried into the street which would take me, so I had hoped, to the water, because by then I had realised that it must be the waters of the Tiber I had been wanting to reach that night.

But I didn't quite reach the waters that night. I could have easily followed Via dei Farnesi, stepped under the arched bridge and reached the river near Ponte Sisto, but somehow, I think, the terrified face of the young girl distracted me. I found myself on Via Monserrato. The street was almost deserted, the silence interrupted by an occasional carriage equipped as usual with the dimmest of lights. Turning left into Vicolo del Malpasso would have taken me past the New Prison to the river but the word prison suddenly obstructed my advance. I decided to walk along Via Giulia, hoping to reach the water near one of my favourite churches. As I went past San Biagio della Pagnotta the bells announced eleven o'clock. I must not wander in the streets so late, I had thought and increased my pace. But then, as it often happens, the most unexpected of things took place; I had just approached the façade of the Palazzo Sacchetti, when I heard the voice. It was coming from an open window on the second floor: a cornetto accompanied by a theorbo and a viola, but soaring above the three, an alto voice. Is that Pietro? I heard myself whisper, still uncertain, but soon I recognised the voice. All of a sudden I felt a shooting pain in my chest that lasted only for a short moment but left me dizzy and weak; I would have collapsed in a heap but for a sudden surge of strength. Meanwhile the voice soared and plunged like a luminous bird weaving strange patterns in the dark air. Crouched against the wet wall I listened and watched, waiting for the song to end. Pietro, my dear boy, I heard myself mumble, raised myself up and walked away slowly, hoping to leave the voice behind. But it came with me to the convent and remained in my head for many days. I am not sure if it will ever leave me now, although it does relax its grip a little when I decide to read or write. But it's also true that I don't really wish it to disappear; I enjoy its company and won't mind if it stays with me a little longer.

***

When I was fourteen, Padre Augustino sent me to learn the art of drawing. I was surprised by the indifference with which Frate Giovanni had welcomed me. He must have known that the excitement I had displayed to learn would vanish after a few weeks and like most other pupils I would soon start looking for something less demanding. Sadly Frate Giovanni was right and the fault, that like others I too had betrayed his trust, I readily admit, lies only with me. Isn't this the fate of every good teacher? An endless sequence of failures. Promises unfulfilled. Hopes deferred. Should I give up as well? The books I have written don't count. No one reads them with the love and understanding they demand. I wait for my Lord to grant me a spiritual son, not a slavish disciple but a fearless companion, to whom I can bequeath the few morsels of knowledge I seem to possess.

Frate Giovanni was a good teacher, a true master of his craft, an honest toiler who believed that only hard labour each day would invoke true benediction. The ease with which he reproduced the likeness of the visible world was indeed uncanny. He had learnt the art in Florence from well-known masters and after many years of practice had perfected the skill. He was conversant with the intricate rules of perspective and the deftness with which he prepared colours and combined them was extraordinary. He had wanted me to learn to draw the human face because according to him there was nothing else more complex or exciting. For the first few days he had told me to draw over and over an oval shape and to add in symmetrical fashion the frontal hair-line, the ears, the nostrils, the arches of the upper and lower lips and the curve representing the chin. But, and this he would reiterate again and again, the most important of all were the eyes. For days I had been forced to draw only the eyes—no face, but almond-like shape with cornea, iris and pupil. Even more time was spent in learning to draw properly the bud-like swellings at the corners, the lashes and the eyebrows, because although these features at first glance might seem to be nothing more

84

than minor details, they were essential to capture the very essence of a human being. The eyes according to him were the mirrors of the spirit, the windows to the soul and the seat of passions. To remember a face, he had counselled, you would have to remember the eyes.

I was able to learn the basics easily and the credit undoubtedly must go to Frate Giovanni, because although there was nothing particularly wrong with my eye-sight, I, and I am sure Frate Giovanni knew it as well, suffered from a perceptible lack of concentration. Why are the eyes so unreliable? Why do they always lead us astray? Why do I have to shut them to remain focused? The answer I soon discovered was rather simple, because our merciful Lord never abandons us completely. The despair he sends us is momentary because if He decides sometimes to deprive us of His benevolence He is more than willing to compensate in some other way: *In God is my salvation and my glory: He is the God of my help, and my hope is in God.*

I realised very early that I was blessed, when as a little child I would run to the ruins of the monastery on the hill top and sit or lie down on the ground, shut my eyes and listen to the noises the world around me made. In the beginning I felt lost, unable to make any sense of the sounds, so diverse and abounding, but slowly I found my way by letting my ears adjust; my mind did the rest. The joy that followed was immense and my gratitude to the Lord unbound. To remember a thing I no longer needed to see it; a noise was enough to etch a trace in my memory. This however doesn't mean that I totally discarded the power of sight; it just became an extension of the main apparatus. The need to hear and listen became critical for me; even written words had to be read aloud, only then was their meaning understood without loss or corruption. Was I doomed forever? I don't think so, because our merciful Lord knows the full extent of our predicament; perhaps that is why He doesn't hesitate for a moment to come to our assistance. The damp air in the cold prison cells could have impaired my hearing forever, but my Lord took care to shield me from the damage; from Him came the bounty and only He had the power to keep it undiminished. I am not young any more and aches in my left ear trouble me often but the skill, I know, hasn't disappeared altogether.

***

It is just past midnight and in the morning when the sun rises it won't be bright and glorious as it always is, because an hour before the noon the moon will cast its shadow on the sun and cover it completely, leaving merely a bright rim. It will last only for a minute or less but for that minute it will turn into a black disc. A fearsome sight. So fearsome that even Santissimo Padre has lost his poise. The rumours of his impending death have frightened him. The word has spread that a group of unholy magicians have performed rituals and summoned oracles pronouncing his demise. I have been commissioned to perform the rites to remedy the situation, to disable the evil influences of Mars and Saturn, and to turn the affection of the unholy magic harmless.

We have sealed the room from the outside air; the rose-vinegar has been sprinkled and the smell of burnt laurel, myrtle, rosemary and cypress fills the room. On the walls hang the long stripes of white silk decorated with leaves and branches of olives and pines. In the middle of the room two tall candles and five torches are lit. They are the seven planets rescued from the heavens in turmoil from the eclipse. When the heavens turn dark, in the lights of the candles and torches they will find a semblance of their luminous presence. On the floor we have etched the ecliptic, marking the path along which the Sun will come face to face with its own brief moment of extinction. We know that it will emerge unscathed as it always has, but the doubts persist. What if the Sun were to disappear forever? What if its re-emergence were to be delayed for a very, very long time? How would the world survive?

Along the ecliptic Angelo Ferrinni has painted signs. From east to west—the Leo, the Cancer, the Gemini and the Pisces at the end. In the centre, just to the left of the Gemini, is Santissimo Padre's own Taurus, majestic, strong and invincible. Some twenty paces away from the ecliptic stands the Cappella. It follows the arcuate shape etched on the floor. A cantus for Mercury, an altus each for Earth and Venus, a tenor for Mars, and two basses—a basso profundo for Saturn and a basso cantante for Jupiter. For the Sun I have decided to mix two voices singing in harmony—a quintus and a youthful treble. The Sun never ages, remains young, fresh and invigorating. The voices are to be assisted by a lute, harpsichord, viola, and a cornetto. Three boys dressed in gold, silver and aquamarine gowns stand at the eastern end of the ecliptic ready to walk slowly: the two hold torches and the one dressed in a gold-coloured gown has a large candle with a bright orange-yellow flame.

Luigi Jolli has composed the music for the ceremony and I am glad that he has listened to my advice. He has created a score which if played and sung properly will produce consonant music, an agreeable harmony of variable pitch and volume—not too shrill or loud so as to cause alarm and not too low and soft as to become inaudible. I have realised that low sounds bruise, condense and thicken the spirit whereas the high ones rarefy and lacerate, hence a careful fusion of the two is essential to establish harmony between celestial and earthly spirits. Following the rules proposed by the Venetian maestro Claudio Monteverdi, the words will be sung and recited in homophonic mode; they and the voices will reign supreme with instruments only providing a congenial background.

Santissimo Padre raises his right hand, palm open, and the ceremony begins. The boy in the golden gown sings; the style is new to me although I have heard and read about it. Jacopo Peri calls it *diastimatica*: sustained and suspended recitation, lying somewhere between the slow and suspended movement of song and the swift and rapid movement of speech. '*O sol che sani ogne vista turbata*,' (*O Sun that clears the mists*) the boy sings, holding the candle in his hand unlit, calling the Sun to appear and light the candle. The viola sounds hushed grumbles, the lute then takes over and a cold shiver runs through my body. How many times before I have read to myself these lines of *Inferno*, I remember thinking, and yet now, in the voice of the young boy they sound so mournful and yet resonant; a strange mixture of hope and despair, of belief and unbelief.

The boy was just ten or perhaps twelve, I wondered at the time, and the voice so blessed, floating like a ball on a water jet. The 'o' of 'sol' and 'ogne' perfectly round, riding on a controlled but sensuous vibrato; the sound a little rough but pleasant like the striated surface of a plum kernel. The lips I recall imagining, and behind them a tongue shaped like a spoon. Control yourself, I had scolded myself as sweat began to moisten my temple and the end of my spine. The sweat was cold and I could feel the big mole above my right nostril twitch. Go away, you devil, I had mumbled. My right hand reached my skull searching for the bumps. I was nervous and began to lose track of the ceremony, which to my great surprise ended without any visible disruption.

"Pietro Manchini," Luigi Jolli would later tell me his name. "From Napoli," he added after a pause. His hesitation to name the cursed city didn't escape my attention. Perhaps I should stop condemning the city and concede that the Spanish occupation hasn't quite vanquished the Neapolitan spirit—wild, free and rebellious. The Spanish don't want me there, perhaps that is why I want to return—to look straight in their eyes and laugh. To annoy them would give me satisfaction although I know that it might come at a heavy price. If my Lord has planted the seed of rebellion in my heart why shouldn't I cherish it and display it?

A year or less later I saw Pietro again at a ceremony in the palazzo of Don Taddeo Barberini, the favourite nephew of Santissimo Padre. His eighteen-month-old son Carlo was threatened by a bad influx. I had looked at the horoscope and was convinced that he had to be shielded from the ill influence of Saturn. The ceremony was less elaborate but it was followed by a short presentation of ariettas, madrigals and canzonettes accompanied by gravicembalo, lira grande and a lute. That night Pietro didn't only sing but played on an ivory cornetto as well. How nicely the voice and the cornetto blend, I had thought then, watching every tiny movement the boy made. The difference soon became obvious; the boy's whole body, particularly his face, altered with each note he sang or played, whereas the cornetto without his breath was listless, a mere instrument waiting to be played. That he was trying hard was quite clear but it was a labour of love, the sole purpose of which was to give pleasure by bringing us face to face with beauty. How infinite, I remember telling myself, is our Lord's benevolence; to create a boy of perfect beauty and disposition, to bless him with such vocal cords and to confer on him at this tender age such impeccable control and discipline. The bewilderment with which Maestro Jolli watched him breathe in and out and carry on the breath phrases littered with complicated vowels was immense. The whole vocal apparatus, he had assured me repeatedly afterwards, worked in such perfect consonance that one day the boy would surely turn into a virtuoso artist.

Later Luigi Jolli would tell me several times that the boy was looking for a suitable place in the Capella Sistina and that it would be nice if I were to whisper a few favourable words in the holy ears of Santissimo Padre. Such was the magic of his voice that I had foolishly acquiesced.

Yes foolish I was, convinced that finally the fate was about to smile in my direction, that once my proposal to establish Collegio Barberino in Rome was accepted a life of meagre comforts would ensue. The wanderings would end and I would be able to finish the books I have left unfinished. I guess the age and infirmity associated with it had caught up with me. I was sixty or so and although I knew that my time was coming to an end, I had prayed to our Lord to bless me at least another ten, just ten, more years to tie up the loose ends: *Have mercy on me, O Lord, for I am weak: heal me, O Lord, for my bones are troubled.*

That I remember him so well, his face, body, his whole beautiful self, even now, this is only because his cornetto-like voice still rings in my ears. There he is, the face a perfect heart-shape; nose straight with a slight upturned curve near the tip, almond-shaped eyes rimmed by arched brows, eyelids heavy, lips succulent of the colour of ripe pomegranate seeds, and chin smooth and soft asking to be touched and kissed. A little crescent scar just above the left cheekbone doesn't sully the immaculate beauty but makes it rather kind, accessible and comforting. A boy he is but dressed in an appropriate costume, with his face painted so very slightly, he can easily pass for a pretty girl.

As I walked home after the ceremony at the palazzo of Don Taddeo Barberini I couldn't stop wondering that I had seen a face of similar beauty elsewhere. For weeks the thought disturbed me and my memory, which I have been so proud of, didn't stop playing hide and seek with me. My frustration grew, and realising that I would have to solve the puzzle soon I decided to ask for help from my dear friend Abram Levi. He heard my description with interest, looked at me with alarm, surprised I think by the anxiety I displayed, and pleaded that he needed a couple of days to make inquiries. We met after three days outside the shop of an art dealer not far from Piazza San Luigi. The little shop was located on the second floor of a building dwarfed by the grand Palazzo Farnese. The stairway was narrow and dark but the shop itself was bright because of the large window. Abram Levi whispered something to the art dealer, an old man with a black pad covering his left eye. The old man looked at me and I noticed that there were two large burn marks on the left side of his face. He asked us to be seated, went inside a small room at the back and came out with three or four unframed paintings. He didn't have the originals, he told us, but the copies were as good, painted by one of the talented apprentices of the great master. Caravaggio, I heard myself mumble and saw a friendly smile appear on the scarred face of the art dealer. Abram Levi grabbed one of the paintings, walked up to the window and pointed at the cupid boy sitting behind the young lutenist in the painting. At last the puzzle was solved but the relief I felt was momentary because it was, I am confident, a mere coincidence that Pietro and the cupid boy were so alike. The same boy was peeling fruit in the second painting but it's the third that I remember most vividly; it was called *Saint Francis of Assissi in Ecstasy* and showed the boy as an angel looking at Saint Francis of Assissi. The old man was intrigued by our keen interest and asked if we were prepared to see something a little naughty. He glanced in the direction of Abram Levi and without waiting for my response pulled out from behind a pile of unframed canvases a small piece, asked us to move closer to the window, and unfurled it, confident that it would leave us speechless. It did and if

I remember it correctly the original too had a similar effect on me.

I had seen the original many years before; it was kept behind a silk curtain and disrobed only for a few selected visitors. I am not sure why I had been accorded that privilege then but the copy in the art dealer's shop clearly unsettled me. No, not this one, I protested and the canvas was swiftly whisked away. The innocent boy, so playfully naked in *Amor Vincit Omnia* had no likeness of Pietro. None at all. Abram Levi was startled by the vehemence with which I had uttered the words 'not this one' and 'none at all' but he was too kind to burden me with more questions. Before saying good-bye that evening, he apologised for causing discomfort and possibly pain and suggested that it would be wise to forget the incident forever. Forget. How easy the word sounds but how very difficult it is to force ourselves not to remember. The pleasurable we forget with ease but the painful lives forever. Why so, my Lord? Why?

In the course of the following few years I met Pietro several times and with each meeting my fascination for him steadily grew. Am I witnessing the advent of a genius? I would ask myself often. If I feel so drawn to him is this because my Lord wants it to be that way? Not to interfere but to nurture with care and compassion. Was it friendship? I am sure it wasn't, because what sort of friendship could ever arise between a young boy and such a decrepit old and ugly mess? Selfishness. Perhaps there was a hint of that; not selfishness exactly but self-interest perhaps. For a child like him it was excusable; he was innocent and eager to succeed; but how did I allow myself to fall prey to such a base and loathsome desire? The piety and humility with which I had lived my long and torturous life had withered in just a few years. A whirlwind had descended and swept me off my feet. I had failed my Lord and failed Pietro and myself: *I am poured out like water; and all my bones are scattered. My heart has become like wax melting in the midst of my bowels.*

I confess that I was blinded by the beauty of the innocent boy. I shouldn't have been, because the beauty was undoubtedly Yours; he was just a vessel into which You had poured Yourself fully and without blemish. I know this now but then face to face with Pietro I had somehow lost sight of the most obvious. Yes, a fool I was, helpless and pathetic. As I utter these words, sorrowful as they are, I do realise that I am trying in vain to find an excuse. Words and more words. But please, my Lord, allow me to confess the sin because although there is nothing hidden from You, I have to nonetheless avow the unavowable. To expiate myself I confess; to redeem my soul I confess; to remain vigilant of future indiscretions I confess; I confess because I am nothing but human asking for love and compassion.

Many years ago, whilst imprisoned in Castel Saint Elmo, I had, I don't know how, found the inspiration to compose a few sonnets. Ordinary and naïve, Dante would have called them, but who can ever match his brilliance? Yes, the imperfections were plenty and all too clear, but they did contain a few metaphors which even Dante would have found engaging.

The sonnet that came closest to perfection was called *Nel Teatro del Mondo*; the spontaneity with which it arrived surprises me even now. It must have been sitting inside, ripening slowly, waiting for the right moment. I wrote it down amazed that I didn't have to alter a single word; it was impeccable in rhyme, rhythm and consonance of thoughts and feelings. I have since then discovered that a famous actor in far-away England has composed on his own something similar but my sonnet, the experts contest, is more delicate, imbued with both irony and lament in right proportions.

I am not sure if they are right but Luigi Jolli was impressed by the sonnet and perhaps that is why it took him so little time to set it to music. He was adamant that the sonnet was meant to be recited and not sung, and that the three instruments he had chosen—a lute, a viola and my favourite cornetto—would achieve it to perfection. I don't know if I agreed with him but he is an expert and knows his music well. Moreover he had at that time managed to play it once or twice to a talented student of Frescobaldi and obtained his approval. He was thrilled and asked me if I had a singer in mind whose voice could do justice to the sonnet and the score. Pietro, I wanted to say, but I didn't have to because Luigi had already asked Pietro to look at the score. He apologised for failing to seek my prior approval but I didn't see any reason to fault him or his choice. We were convinced, he more than I, that Pietro would make the sonnet survive the onslaught of time; that touched by the voice of a genius it would fail to die. Luigi was craving for immortality and to be honest I too was seduced by the idea. Did I have any qualms or misgivings? I surely had, because the conceit of the whole enterprise was utterly shameful, but I was blinded by greed and insolence had crippled my heart. A state of paralysis had dawned and the will to resist and react had deserted me. I was doomed.

How easy it is, my Lord, to forget the simple lessons the everyday life throws our way. Like an ignorant child we easily misplace our bearings and allow ourselves to be carried away by the currents of deceitful thoughts. We are driftwood in the sea, hoping that the kind hand of our merciful Lord will rescue us but the Lord has given us minds to think and will to act freely; perhaps that is why He expects us to be responsible and to pay for misjudgments and errors of action and inaction; He sends us pain and suffering so that we the arrant creatures will one day learn to live properly, but unfortunately, or perhaps fortunately, life is too short.

Solace, I admit with profound sadness, comes from the thought that I am not alone; that there are others who too have failed. Even Santissimo Padre, I hate to record, has faltered on several occasions. I know well how ardently he has patronised Cavaliere Bernini, hoping that one day he will cast in marble a likeness of him more marvellous than the now famous bust of Cardinal Scipione Borghese. Bernini is magnificent and some rightly believe more talented than Michelangelo Buonarroti. I have seen the two *Davids* and there is no doubt in my mind that the *David* of Michelangelo is inferior in many ways; he is imposing I concede but seems entombed inside the beautiful marble. Bernini's *David* on the other hand is teeming with energy, ready to shatter the marble and launch himself at his detractors. Glorious I call this *David*, glorious and glorifying. Now I know why Santissimo Padre isn't very pleased with the portrait Bernini did a few years ago. In it Santissimo Padre looks insipid and withdrawn. The marble bust in the Basilica di San Pietro too hasn't quite satisfied him. I have heard that the bronze bust ready to be unveiled next year may do the trick and bring joy to both Bernini and Santissimo Padre.

I have met Bernini only a few times, otherwise I would have warned him about the capriciousness with which Reverendissimo Padre looks at such things. He isn't very easy to please, I know it well, and when pleased he doesn't readily display it. The commendations he offers are often muted and veiled. Many years ago I was asked to read his poems and suggest edits and alterations. Some of the poems were truly remarkable but most were nothing but pale imitations of Virgil, Petrarch and Dante. I was advised to be vigilant and keep my criticism carefully veiled. In the end I agreed to write a rather lengthy commentary, just to facilitate an easy comprehension of the work. As expected they were appreciated and I was fortunate that my effort remained un-noticed; it's much safer that way because who knows in what form misfortune will strike.

Santissimo Padre loves nature and some of his best poems reflect a desire to express the thrill he experiences encountering its unsullied beauty. But then he is also very pragmatic; he has to be, otherwise why would he have ordered all the birds in the Vatican gardens to be trapped and killed? The poor birds disturbed his sleep, someone had explained to me a few years later.

***

Al Signor Galileo Galilei,

The news has come that you have finally reached home and although you aren't able to enjoy full freedom yet, the danger of further persecution has subsided. I am pained to hear that you have been afflicted with severe hernia and that your request to summon a doctor from Rome has been refused. Terrible times, my dear friend, terrible and unfortunate. I hope you aren't offended by this informal address. I have always considered you a dear and close friend and although I have in the past few years tried deliberately to avoid meeting you or writing to you, I am more than ever sure that you, my esteemed friend, know and appreciate the reasons. The times are such, my friend, that it would be wise to avoid any contact or communication because we may unwittingly cast dark shadows of suspicion and ill fate on each other. Perhaps that is why although I am writing this letter to you I am not certain if I will find the courage to send it to you. It will remain unfinished, and if finished remain uncommunicated, safely lodged with my other papers and documents. If in case I decide to send this letter, my humble advice would be to read it and destroy it soon after. I shall go even a step further by suggesting that it would be more prudent to mislay any remembrance of this audacious and at times erratic submission.

However let me begin with one of my most cherished memories, because try as I may I can't forget the beautiful sunny day when a packet from our dear friend Antonio Persio was delivered to me. The year was 1612 and I was into the fourth year of a six-year period of limited, or as was described to me then, carefully monitored freedom. The packet had a palm-size *Book of Hours* exquisitely illuminated by a Dutch painter and printed with love and care in Rotterdam by a Jewish master. It warmed my heart and I carried it in my pocket for months. The joy I felt was immense but I am sure you would believe me if I were to say that even greater pleasure issued from holding another book; this one was of rather humble appearance and the cover had suffered minor damage on the way. It was, my dear friend, your own *Sidereus Nuncius*; the title, I had immediately thought then, was most appropriate because the message which *The Starry Messenger* brought was exciting beyond any belief. I was in the midst of finishing a short pamphlet inspired by Plato and Saint Augustine's *City of God*. I had to put it away to concentrate on the reading and comprehension of your new ideas. Although I had already heard much about them, reading directly the narrative of your quest to solve the mysteries of the celestial world was audacious as well as inspirational; the text so lucid guided only by the urgency to make the chain of thoughts as clear as possible, interspersed with your drawings, simple but illuminating precisely the description of what your sharp eyes had observed with the assistance of that marvellous instrument of yours, the telescope. Our Lord's blessing is boundless, I said to myself repeatedly then. He first inspired you to invent such an extraordinary instrument and then instilled in you immense patience and power of concentration to observe tirelessly the infinite realm of the stars so mysteriously and exquisitely designed by Him.

After reading *The Starry Messenger*, I couldn't look at the night sky as I had done before; it had changed and I suppose I too had changed. The moon I began to see then became a copy of your wondrous drawings with mountains, valleys and volcanic craters. The perfection of shape, I concluded, to which Aristotle had given undue significance was a miscalculation, a wishful dream and like all dreams unreal. It's not the perfection of shape which I think defines the being of the worldly and celestial entities but the hidden vitality infused in them. Telesio reasoned that it emanates from the eternal conflict between the two opposite principles fighting for self-preservation. For Ficino the vitality was the *spiritus mundi* flowing through the sensible world. But let me not tire you with my not-so-clear ramblings about the metaphysical world. For an eminent student of natural philosophy these may appear nothing more than figments of a confused imagination. Metaphysics is critical, I do believe, and without it life, I am sure, would lose its moral bearings. But I also believe that for metaphysics to be relevant, it needs to be guided by the understanding obtained from a thorough and precise examination of the natural world. The same I think is true of theology; it too needs to discover its basis in natural philosophy, otherwise it will remain obscure and uncertain of its proper purpose.

I am astounded by the ingenuity with which you have transformed the toy glass of the Dutch maker of spectacles into a device that can produce upright images of bodies twenty and more times larger than their actual size, but more amazing I think is your other optical device, a kind of Janus-like sibling of the telescope. With it you have turned your gaze on the more immediate world, not as luminous as the celestial bodies, but intriguing and mysterious nonetheless. The drawings of dead flies, beetles and fishes, which I was fortunate enough to see in your book in a shop a few years ago, were marvellous. I am told that the tube of this wonderful apparatus contains two lenses of doubly convex shapes, the grinding of which, I gather, would have taken much effort and application.

I am confident that devices of this kind will allow us to reveal the inner being of things; they will augment the power of the naked eye and permit us to discover the intricate details, essential for their existence. The world is mysterious but the mysteries aren't hidden from us; one only needs the guiding hand of an enlightened soul like yours to resolve their inherent logic. We will soon realise that the naked eye can't be trusted anymore, and that to comprehend the nature of truth it is essential to cross the boundary of the visible, and dare I say, the sentient world. I do believe that the natural world isn't only vast in its dimensions but quite complicated in the make-up of its constituents. But more importantly instruments and contraptions similar to yours will bring us closer to the true nature of the human body, its flesh, blood and bones, and make us comprehend the mysterious workings of the mind, the spirit and ultimately of the soul.

If our Lord wishes us to know the natural world, and I believe everything in it is knowable, He also wants us to know ourselves. We are part of, and in unity with, the natural world, different but still belonging to the same world. By knowing the world and ourselves we come to know Him. Perhaps that is why I am convinced that Copernican understanding of the celestial world is nothing but a step in our eternal journey to know His ways. The earth we live on isn't at the centre of the celestial sphere, on the surface of which the stars are fixed like buttons, but that the sphere in its dimension is infinitely large, and that if the planets including earth go round the sun as the moon so magnificently does round the earth, and your Stars of Medici do round the Jupiter, can it not be true that the sun itself along with its planets and moons revolves round some yet to be known but knowable body? The celestial world is infinite because our Lord, who is as infinite as the world, has fashioned it so; the infinity of the world emanates and resides in Him.

Cognoscere est sentire. To know means to feel. I have always believed this to be true. Without feeling, without senses, true knowledge is impossible. Perhaps that is why the instruments and devices which you make and apply to look, feel and observe the world, fascinate me. The world acts on us, and we know that it acts, because we feel the modifications that result from it. These modifications are vital because they make us aware of our own existence.

You once mentioned that your revered father wanted you to study medicine and thereby learn the functioning of the body and mind, and through it to understand the ways of healing bodies and spirits, marred by various afflictions. I too entertained a similar aspiration. My visit to Padua was for that purpose only. But before coming to Padua I spent a few months in the enlightened cities of Sienna and Pisa. I can't imagine how my life would have changed if I had obtained a chair in metaphysics at the University of Pisa. I was just twenty-five then and rather overzealous to impress; perhaps that is why I failed. The visits to Florence and Bologna didn't bring much success either. In Bologna I took refuge in the convent of San Domenico but it was a false refuge because the Inquisition wouldn't let me leave without handing over all my finished and unfinished manuscripts. They were lost forever. I realised then that I had been marked and that I wouldn't ever be able to escape the dark shadows of the Inquisition. That they were after me became quite clear as soon as I arrived in Padua; why else would they lay on me the despicable charge of sodomy? Luckily I found a few friends and sympathisers who agreed to vouchsafe statements in support of my innocence. The whole sordid affair utterly dejected me and I have to confess that there were occasions when I thought of ending my life. It sounds stupid and reckless but can there be anything more evil than despair?

In Padua I met you for the first time and like you became a student. I still miss those days and fondly remember the stimulating discussions we used to have about the nature of worldly and non-worldly phenomena. I gave private lessons in metaphysics and Spanish and attended classes in medicine and anatomical dissections. I wanted to be a special kind of physician; the one who also had a sound knowledge of metaphysics: a rare combination, don't you think? Just imagine a friar who, thanks to the infinite benevolence of our Lord, is capable of healing both, the body and the soul. The conceit hidden in these words does disturb me even now but I don't want to lie. Yes, conceited I truly was. Aren't we all? How foolish the exuberance of youthful years can often be.

You used to play on the lute the songs composed by your eminent father. You had a lovely voice, and I am disappointed that you have given up singing altogether. In the past few years I have read several times *Dialogo Della Musica Antica e Della Moderna* and haven't stopped marvelling at the deep knowledge with which your father writes about music. It has taken me time but now I am beginning to comprehend clearly the nature of his passion for the music, in which the quality of musical sound blends harmoniously with the quality of the spoken word—an organic unison between the two. Music not just for puerile entertainment but also for the nourishment of the human and non-human spirit.

Music does touch us, we know that well, causing apprehensible modifications in the physical and emotional state of our being. Ficino's explanation was rather crude and I don't agree with him that it is because music is transmitted by animated air, the same substance which also fills our ears, the *spiritus aerus*, to use his words. It is as silly as the suggestion which Aristotle made to explain the working of the human eye; the eye he had said was filled with transparent and hence luminous fluid. But I do agree with Ficino that music through emotions affects the senses and the soul and by meaning it works on the mind.

Do you remember the three anatomical dissections we witnessed in the surgical theatre at the University? We were lucky, I had thought then, otherwise how could we have seen in one day anatomical sections of the larynx and the glottis of three singers: a ten-year old boy with a beautiful cantus voice, a female soprano and, most marvellous of all, a thirty-or-so-year-old castrato. His name was Vincenzo Vittori and they say he had a voice as luscious as Signora Vittoria Archieri. At nineteen, I am told, he possessed the grace of a young woman and the brash but endearing demeanour of a young bull; he was tall and thin and was draped in luminous skin that glowed like Chinese silk. When he sang you couldn't take your eyes off him; even to miss a moment was considered a great misfortune. Although at times one could hear the shrill and acidulous tones of a falsettist, everyone marvelled at the clarity of timbre and the sheer piercing power of his voice; it soared, plummeted, scooped and could hold notes for unimaginably prolonged duration without ever pausing for breath.

As I looked at him lying dead on the table, mutilated by the sharp knife of the assassin, I couldn't believe that this was the body that had just a few months earlier given such pleasure to so many people. The assassin was a jealous lover unable to contain his or her passion. Why his or her, because as you know, no one was certain about the true identity of the killer. Some had even come to believe that he or she was a castrato of average talent but with patronage. The body had thirty wounds—one for every single year of his eventful life, someone had remarked—but the main wound was in the abdominal region just below the diaphragm. His face had been slashed and deformed beyond recognition. The blood from the wounds had blocked the trachea and crusted over the larynx. The larynx, we were astounded to discover, was rather small with vocal cords slightly bigger than that of the female soprano. The conclusion was obvious: a large resonating chamber—the diaphragm, the pharynx, the nasal and oral cavities—was the principle source of his spectacular voice. I know I am simplifying the complexity, because the beauty of the voice isn't only determined by the perfection of the physical apparatus; the nurturing of appropriate spirit is even more essential, and that comes from years and years of exercise and exertion. One needs to attune the ear to the sounds the world around us makes and then practice incessantly to understand and reproduce them without corruption, but most of all one has to acknowledge and rejoice in the boundless benevolence of our Lord who has chosen one of us to listen to His songs and reproduce them.

As I recall the appearance of the dead castrato I can't fail to note the sorrow I felt looking at him. The grace and beauty of his younger years had all but disappeared; he was still exceptionally tall but had become quite obese; his hips were round and fleshy and his shoulders tight and narrow—he wasn't grotesque but there was a certain obscenity in the ugliness, as if nature at the reckoning of our Lord had taken its revenge. Why aren't we ever satisfied with the attributes endowed to us by nature? The quest for perfection is willed to us but why do we forget the simple truth that perfection will only come by growing whatever has been given to us? Instead of careful adjustment and tuning guided by a loving master we opt for a quicker and less tiresome solution. The success often comes, and blinded by the rewards we begin to believe that there wasn't anything wrong with the way we had achieved it; we readily forget that we were driven by conceit and the lure of ephemeral gains; but soon our own body and spirit begin to rebel; the disintegration and decay ensue in rapid succession. If our Lord has given us free will, isn't it because He wants us to recognise the limits of our own humanity and act accordingly? I hope you agree with me that to define the nature of human freedom differently would be disastrous.

Ten years ago I was faced with a similar dilemma, and I feel sad to confess that I didn't quite know the right answer. That I had erred has become abundantly clear to me now, and it's too late for me to do anything other than to admonish myself for not showing enough courage to intervene. I had once again kept quiet and let the events run their course. Disgraceful it was, and I know it well, but what troubles me even more is that it wasn't the first or the last time that I had willed myself not to act.

His name was Pietro, a ten year old boy of immense beauty; a voice so …

I couldn't continue the letter further, overwhelmed with guilt and shame. I didn't rewrite it either. On reading it again I was surprised by its tone. It sounded too confessional and pitiful. To send such a narrative to my esteemed friend would be highly inappropriate, I had decided, but I couldn't bring myself to destroy it. It has remained with me, reminding me of my follies and indiscretions. That I am pitiable and fallible has become abundantly clear to me and I'll keep the flawed submission as a memento.

The letter that I finally sent to Signor Galilei was a short note in which I congratulated him for his safe return and asked him to be a bit more cautious and tactful henceforth. To lose him now, I implored, would be a calamity because the job assigned to him by our Lord isn't finished as yet. I'll pray to the Lord, I wrote, to grant him many more years of pleasant and fruitful labour so that he could enthral us with countless new inventions and discoveries.

***

A few months ago I received a letter from Signor Gabriel Naude. It included a brief account of the progress he had made on the biography he has been writing.

He had approached me with the idea in Napoli, and at the time I tried to dissuade him, calling the undertaking ill-conceived and without merit, although I do admit that I was flattered by the prospect of finding my eventful life recounted on the pages of a book authored by a learned man like him. He was adamant, unwilling to relent, and I didn't want to smother the enthusiasm he had so earnestly displayed.

In Napoli he would visit me in the cell and we would converse for hours. He would take notes and then read them out to confirm that his record didn't contain errors of mishearing or misconception. Both he and I wanted to be careful not to turn the account into a blatant hagiography. To me it soon became evident that I wasn't overly interested in the final outcome of the project; what I wanted most was an interlocutor with whom I could explore the contours of my own becoming. Like shafts of light his questions illumed the dark alleys of my life, revealing moments of which either I had no memory or the significance of which had hitherto remained incomprehensible to me.

My friends have often marvelled at my ability to retain memories of the things past; prodigious they have called it, and I agree that I too have been impressed by the ease with which I can retrieve the past and recreate it without loss or corruption. But conversations with my kind friend revealed that my hold on memories was after all not very strong; that I too had failed to recall the past in its fullness; that I too had to call imagination to lend me a hand. Did my dear friend notice my failings? I am sure he must have.

Perhaps that is why I wasn't surprised by his request. I read his letter with interest and liked the novel form in which he wished me to respond; instead of questions he sent me a list of words and asked me to compose a brief note or a narrative about it. How exciting, I told myself, thrilled with the idea of immersing myself in the game I had always wanted to play but had never got a chance to.

Insanity

They call it *la veglia*, the 'wake'. It went for forty hours, interrupted by short breaks for escorted visits to the latrine, to empty the bowels or to wash off the excrement leaked from lack of control. The 'wake' began early on the morning of the fourth day in June. I was taken inside a special cell hidden in the darkest bowels of Castel Nuovo. My arms were twisted behind my back; my wrists were bound by a rope from which my body, shielded only with a thin sheet of underwear, was suspended a few inches above a seat fitted with sharp wooden spikes. My arms would ache and shoulders give in, unable to keep me suspended, hence I would lower myself on the seat. Just for a minute, I would mumble, just to gather a few morsels of strength; but the spikes would hurt, tearing the flesh, and I would have to look away to avoid the sight of blood.

Giacomo Ferraro, the gaoler, remained with me, keeping vigil during the long forty hours. When the pain became unbearable, I would shout, he had told me later; an amazing mixture of phrases in curial Latin peppered with curses in Italian and Calabrian. "You always curse best in your mother tongue," I had told him and laughed. He had laughed too, admiring the sheer power of Calabrian profanities.

He was a kind man, my gaoler, an honest witness of my suffering. Was he able to feel the pain I endured? I don't know. Perhaps not. Who can?

The torture I knew was an instrument to determine if I was truly insane. A few months before I had set fire to my mattress and started behaving strangely. To escape the death penalty, they must have thought. The 'wake' confirmed that I was insane or at least gave them a chance to declare me so, and hence save me from being burnt alive on the stake. My Lord had willed me to survive and survive I did.

Was I mad to feign insanity so stubbornly? Perhaps I was. But some would say that I wasn't mad at all, just a little too strong-willed. No, I was neither sane nor insane but just listening to the whispers of my Lord urging me to keep faith and persevere: *For He is my God and my saviour; He is my protector.*

Settimontana Squilla

When I was four or perhaps a little older, I somehow found myself perched on the branch of a tree. It wasn't very tall but the loud screams of my mother standing underneath had scared me and I was stuck, unable to come down of my own will.

My father that day had gone to the neighbouring village to purchase leather from a Spanish merchant. I didn't know what to do. My mother was too big and timid to climb herself. Stay there she had ordered and ran away to call my cousin who was swimming in the river. The two returned and found me lying on the ground. I must have slipped and fallen off the tree. At first my mother thought that I was dead but she was wrong; she touched me all over. The touch of her hands is still fresh in my memory. Isn't it strange? She touched me and kissed me and picked me up in her arms to carry me home when I woke up from sleep which wasn't sleep at all but a state of deep shock. But I didn't cry, just looked at her still uncertain of the state I was in, she would tell everyone afterwards. I had a small cut on the left side of my head. She saw the cut, washed the dried blood and then began to smile and laugh, without ever telling me why.

A few days later I heard her whispering to my father, after which the two called me to come up and began to feel my head. The next morning I was taken to a barber and my head was shaved clean. The hair would grow again, my mother consoled me, thicker and darker. By then I had realised that there was something not quite right with my head; my mother couldn't stop laughing and I knew that the unusual thing which had suddenly revealed itself on my scalp wasn't very scary. She asked me if I was curious to find out; I certainly was but I was also a little afraid. She grabbed my right hand, raised my arm and made my fingers move; they were like marbles, round but squishy. We counted them together; three on the left, three on the right and one just near the temple. Mother was convinced that their appearance on my scalp wasn't an accident; they had meaning very much like the words we speak, perhaps, some sort of premonition of my future, full of hope and promise.

That's how I, Giovanni Domenico Campanella, the son of a poor Calabrian cobbler, got the nickname Settimontana Squilla—Seven-hilled Bell.

Ecstasy

Do you remember the Genoese sailor, the principle interlocutor of my poetical dialogue *La Cita del Sole*? Without him I couldn't have written the short book. We spent many days together talking. I am wrong; he did most of the talking, I only listened and took notes. Before taking leave he asked me if I would accept a gift from him. I would be honoured, I replied. The hesitation with which he took the gift out alarmed me a little and I have to confess that the little bronze statue he placed in my hand was shocking. His response was immediate and quite predictable, but I didn't let him put away the statue. In a flash I decided that it wanted to be looked at, touched and discussed.

The sailor told me that he had procured the statue at one of the many bustling ports in southern India. The twelfth century bronze had come from a site in Tamilnadu. It was called *Natraja* or *God Shiva the King of Dance*. To say that I was ignorant about the existence of such so-called sacred artefacts wouldn't be right; I had encountered vivid descriptions of them in the accounts of many travellers, and yet its mere presence in front of my eyes stunned me. Its power was immediate and palpable. I soon noticed that I had started sweating.

The dancing god was crushing with his right foot a dwarf crouched on a lotus. His left leg was raised across his body. He had four hands. One of his right hands, held high with an open palm, was meant to reassure the devotee. The second right hand played on a small hand drum, while one of his left hands, arched like a semi crescent, emanated fire. His legs and four arms conveyed a sense of energetic but blissful dance. So did the hair, flying on both sides, and the long end of the sash. His flying hair seemed like waves of water. In the hair, not far from the hand holding a drum, I could see a tiny figure of a goddess called *Ganga*. The name of one of the five celestial rivers described by Herodotus, I told my interlocutor. Perhaps, was his short reply. Shiva, the *Natraja* was embedded in the centre of a ring of fire. The ring was joined to a tall crown placed on his head. On the forehead, right in the centre, I saw a small, upright, almond-like indention—an eye. The god had three eyes, one less than the Greek god Phanes.

He was the god of death and destruction, the sailor explained. Why is he dancing then? I asked him. Is this an orgy of power? He didn't know, was his reply. He paused for a moment and then asked me if he could show me one more strange piece of stone. He told me that he didn't want to offend me but that the stone would perhaps answer my question. I admired his intrigue. He had trapped me by igniting the flame of curiosity in my heart. Don't worry, I replied, I won't be offended. He repeated his question still unsure of my reaction, but after receiving my approval thrust in my hand a curious piece of carved granite. The phallus-like shape of the object was obvious, but the five faces engraved on it looked mysterious. The three-eyed god, the sailor told me, was also the god of fertility; four of the faces represented the four basic elements: air, water, fire and earth, whereas the fifth, looking up, denoted the sky. The four faces on the four sides had an almond-like eye etched in the centre of the forehead.

Now I know why the three-eyed god of death is dancing, I remember explaining to my interlocutor. He is dancing in ecstasy, because once the god of death has cleared the realms, he will initiate the act of creation. He is dancing in hope and anticipation. He is dancing to celebrate the new beginning, a resurrection perhaps. Like a poet or a musician, he is filled with the timbre of a virgin sound or of a nascent phrase, which rises in him like a cloud, lifting him up, light and joyous. Haven't we all felt this way at least once in our life? I certainly have and the credit for it goes to our merciful Lord.

Sin

I wish you hadn't included this awful word in the list. But you have and I know that you want me to respond. So here it is then, the story—short, miserable and absolutely true.

It happened in Napoli. I had come out of the monastery that night to look at the late evening sky. I had, after a prolonged search, discovered a secluded place on the top of the hill from where I was able to watch the sky undisturbed and make notes of my observations. I would spread a blanket on the flattened rocks and lie down to look. It was the month of July and the sky was lighted by the red Mars, bright and clear. For the three previous nights thick clouds had masked the sky, testing my patience. On the fourth night the sky remained clear for many hours, allowing me to enjoy the full glory of the star-lit sky. Tired by the thrill and exertion I must have gone to sleep. I don't recall for how long, but I clearly remember hearing some one cry. I woke up and the cry, I realised soon, was real. I got up and looked around waiting to ascertain the source. I didn't have to wait long because I soon heard a loud shout of a woman coming from the direction of the shepherd's hut I had walked past. It wasn't more than a few hundred paces down from the hill top. Go, the voice inside me told me, and I went down the track to discover the most ugly sight.

They were three. I could see them clearly—three young novices from the monastery. I had seen them occasionally in the library and the garden, always together, whispering to each other. The woman was a girl of fourteen or a little older. One of the three men, pressing her down on the ground, had put his hand on her mouth while another was violating her. After he had finished, the other two took his place. The misery however didn't end there because they soon turned her over and sodomised her one by one. Now they will leave her in peace, I had thought, but I was wrong. One of them, the youngest of the three, the one with an innocent face of a cherub, took a rock lying on the ground and smashed her face, not once but three times. It was only then did they notice that they were being watched. The one with the rock in his hand looked at me, made a hissing sound, trying to scare me. He was about to throw the rock at me, when the tallest of the three pushed him aside. The young man dropped the rock, barked something in the direction of his cohorts, and the three quickly lowered the cowls over their faces and fled. The young man with the rock didn't have to hiss to frighten me because I was, I honestly confess, scared beyond belief. Scared and stunned. It must have taken me a few moments to apprehend the situation but as soon as I saw the crushed face of the young girl my legs gave in and I fell on the ground. I wept and howled like little children often do, trying in vain to pull the sky down. After a short while I raised myself, walked up to the mutilated body of the young girl and without looking at her, lowered the wet blanket over her.

Back in the monastery, I went to see Frate Bernardo, the doctor. He heard my story and without saying a word walked with me back to the site of the terrible crime. The young girl was already dead. The moon above our heads was big and bright, shamelessly shedding light as if nothing untoward had happened under its celestial gaze.

No one in the monastery saw the three novices again.

Is there any need for me to ask whose sin was greater? The answer, my dear friend, is obvious. They were driven by lust, but what about me? Why did I stand and watch the sordid act again and again? Why? Why didn't I try to stop them? Why?

Grace

Let me tell you about a fir, a tree like which I have never again seen in my whole life. No, I have come across many firs, pines, junipers and spruces but this was a special tree, as if made just for me. I don't know how and why it suddenly graced my life with its sudden appearance, but I do remember clearly the day when I first laid my eyes on this beautiful creature. I was fifteen and had developed a habit of taking long walks in the forest. On these walks I would talk to myself, relaxed I think by the unhurried rhythms of the natural world, but the content of my ramblings, was rather trivial because I don't remember anything of significance about them.

One afternoon it had started raining and I took shelter under a leafy chestnut. It was late in August and the autumn was at its peak. Sitting under the tree I saw on the opposite bank of the river a fir, tall and mighty, standing alone amongst sweet chestnuts, reluctantly shedding leaves. The late afternoon sun was behind the tree, and the light refracted by the moist air had created a rainbow-like halo; as if the tall conical shape had just descended from the luminous sky, eager to breathe new life into everything scattered around it; God's will and grace I must have thought then, so omnificent and magnanimous. But the true meaning of the word grace I discovered later, when after an hour's walk across the river I touched the dark grey bark of the giant fir—rough, warm and resinous. Surrounded by the stony walls of the prison cell, I would will myself to recreate a semblance of the same touch—perhaps to convince myself that there still was some hope that I might survive the ordeal; that my Lord hadn't abandoned me forever; that He was watching over me, asking me to wait for the right moment.

The ground around the fir was covered in leaves, needles, cones and shreds of bark. The moist air warmed by the sun had initiated slow decay but the smell was strangely pleasant. The grass was littered with red and brown chestnuts, their oily shells shining like bright beads. I took off my shoes and walked bare-feet a few hundred paces; the touch was exquisite; at first a cold shiver shot through my body, but slowly a state of calmness descended, drowning me deep, as if in the waters of a tranquil lake. I decided to sit down; my pulse had slowed and my mind was emptied of thoughts and intentions; for a few minutes it felt as if I had ceased to exist. Luckily it didn't last long. Why luckily? Because the feeling of being not alive and still remaining conscious of that sensation, wasn't only new but quite unnerving as well.

I would visit the fir, yes, 'visit' is the right word, often, and slowly discover the plenitude of life coexisting with it; it followed an intricate logic of interdependence—harsh perhaps, but not cruel, controlled merely by necessity rather than greed. I was startled by the rational design of this living world at the centre of which stood the tall fir. It didn't take me long to understand that the fir itself was part of something larger and more intricate.

I once managed to climb up the fir to look inside the hollows and found in one a few eggs guarded jealously by a beautiful owl. She smiled at me with her glassy eyes and then ignored me completely. I soon discovered that the squirrels were more brave and adventurous. There was a pair that seemed to wait for me, wanting to be fed. I also saw a few snakes and was lucky that they chose to show no interest in my presence. There were ants and worms, birds and bees, fungi and lichen and, most surprising of all, large spiders hanging from the branches, weaving their delicate webs.

I am sure you don't want me to explain what the word 'grace' has to do with the giant fir. Any further explanation, you know well, would make my narrative redundant. The wings the words span isn't limitless; often they fail to fly and it would be prudent to remain cognisant of their failure; if they cause infliction, the cure for it resides in close proximity to them, and the cure, my dear friend, is silence.

Yes, just silence.

***

Three days after *lunedi di Pasque*, Luigi Jolli came to visit me at the convent. He brought news about Pietro and the news wasn't good. It confirmed my suspicion. Pietro had changed. The lure of fame and wealth had clouded his judgment. He was too young to judge, I thought to myself, too innocent to understand the full implications of his decision. Now it was too late to undo the damage. Yes, it was foolish, but according to Luigi, new doors had opened for him; his name was being mentioned and some composers had begun writing songs for him. Soon he would receive an invitation from Venice to sing for Monteverdi, who loves young castrato voices especially of contralto register. Luigi tried to reassure me that the word about Venice and Monteverdi wasn't a mere rumour and that one of his reliable informants in the beautiful city had verified the news. We should pray for him, he told me, and pray I would because he would definitely need the healing touch of our Lord's gracious hand.

The meeting didn't last long and one of the reasons was the vow of silence I had imposed on myself. I hadn't spoken a word aloud for forty five days and although I continued to whisper silently to myself, I had tried hard to fight that urge as well. The thoughts, I decided, would enter my mind not wordless but as words without sounds; that I would practice the art of silent reading, and with time, the thought, hidden amongst the words, would trickle noiselessly into my mind and unravel its intricate details as a blessing.

There was one other reason behind my silence. Although I feel ashamed for doubting the friendship and loyalty which Luigi harbours for me, I wasn't quite sure that I should tell him about the letter which I had a few days before received from the French ambassador. The best way to keep the plan secret was to stay quiet; even a word accidentally uttered would have opened the floodgates. My anxiety to remain quiet didn't escape his attention. He is far too perceptive to miss it but he knows that if I have chosen to keep silent about certain things, there must be reason for it. His kindness to me is beyond any doubt and I am confident that no harm will ever ensue from him. When the time is right, he'll know whatever he needs to. He'll understand and forgive me.

It has been conveyed to me that Santissimo Padre himself wants me to leave Rome and an agreement between him and the French ambassador has been reached to allow me to escape. The hatred the Spanish feel for me is well known and I have to confess that the feeling is mutual and not without basis. The recent arrest of Piganelli, my so-called disciple, has fuelled their suspicion and ill-will. It is decided that I will travel to Livorno in the carriage of the ambassador under a false name and with false papers, board a French ship and sail to Marseilles. A room has been found for me in the Dominican convent on the Rue Saint Honore. The room is spacious, with large windows and delightful views of the gardens and the Seine. I'll be able to read and write to my heart's content, that's what I have been told. They want me to finish the unfinished manuscripts, to revise the old and to begin working on new ideas. Their enthusiasm alarms me. I doubt if I have the will and energy to do whatever they expect from me. Let me live in peace, I want to tell them. I am old and want to rest. Most of my books are cumbersome and rather difficult to read. The ideas they contain are unclear and the logic muddled. Only one book, *La Cita del Sole*, has given me some satisfaction and I hope it finds a place in the loving hearts of a few readers.

Perhaps I should ask my friends to reprint it with a few illuminations, just to make the reading a little easier. Only fifty or so of my poems have survived. There was a time when I was very proud of my memory to keep the traces of my words alive, boasting that I could reproduce them at will and without loss of content. I should have been more humble and penned them down. It's too late now, but it does hurt and not only because I am really quite fond of them. The emotions they evoke are true, perhaps that's why I like them more than the prosaic works baulking under the weight of abstract metaphysical thoughts.

Before leaving, Luigi asked me to write something on the back of his book of hours. I hesitated for a few moments, still uncertain if it would be a proper way to break the vow of silence I had promised to continue for fifteen more days. Finally I decided that I would write just two words, taking care not to whisper or read them aloud.

The words were: *Consumatum est (It is finished)*.

Luigi read the words and somehow understood that he should resist the temptation to voice them aloud, kneeled down, kissed my hand, and walked outside without even once looking back.

I saw him walking down the corridor and concluded that he had understood the meaning of the two short words. This was going to be our last meeting. That's it. No more.

Dear friend, you should know that in the last few days a voice inside me is whispering without respite the seven fateful utterances of Jesus on the cross. They appear and disappear in no particular order and I am unable to comprehend the full import of their unwavering presence. Perhaps I am nervous to take leave and go into exile. Perhaps I am apprehensive of the uncertain future. Perhaps.

And the voice doesn't stop whispering:

Deus meus, Deus meus, utquid dereliquisti me? (My God, My God, why hast thou forsaken me?);

Sitio (I thirst);

Consummatum est (It is finished);

In manus tuas, Domine, commendo spiritum meum (Into thine hands, O Lord, I resign my spirit);

And again:

Consummatum est. (It is finished).

Acknowledgments

Kabir's poem "Rain clouds gather and darken" is taken from Vinay Dharwadker, *Kabir: The Weaver's Song*. Penguin Books India, New Delhi, 2003. Tommaso Campanella's poem "Nel Teatro del Mondo", quoted from the Project Gutenberg Ebook of Sonnets by Michael Angelo Buonarroti & Tommaso Campanella. Downloaded from the website http:// www.gutenberg.org/files/10314/10314-8.txt in May 2006.

In writing these monologues I have consulted many sources, the most significant of which include: Hajari Prasad Dwivedi, *Kabir*, Rajkamal Prakashan, New Delhi, 1971 (in Hindi); *The Bijak of Kabir*, Translated by Linda Hess and Sukhdeo Singh, Oxford University Press, New York, 2002; Harvey Pitcher, *Chekhov's Leading Lady: A Portrait of the Actress Olga Knipper*. John Murray, London, 1979; Chekhova, M. P., *Iz Dalekogoa Proshlogoa* [*From the Deep Past*]. Khudozhestvennaya Literatura, Moskva, 1960 [In Russian]; Donald Rayfield, *Anton Chekhov: A Life*. Harper Collins, London, 1997; A. V. Khanilo, "M. P. Chekhova—the founder and the first director of House-Museum A. P. Chekhov in Yalta", *In* Kuleshov. V. E. et al (eds). *The Chekhov Readings in Yalta*. Kniga, Moskva, 1973 [In Russian]; Yu. P. Blagovolina, "The History of House-Museum in Yalta: based on the Materials in the Lenin State Library of USSR", *In* Kuleshov. V. E. et al (eds). *The Chekhov Readings in Yalta*. Kniga: Moskva, 1973 [In Russian]; Tommaso Campanella, *La Citta del Sole: Dialogo Poetico* [*The City of the Sun: A Poetical Dialogue*], Translated with Introduction and notes by Daniel J. Donno, University of California Press, Berkley, 1981; Bernardino M. Bonansea, *Tommaso Campanella: Renaissance Pioneer of Modern Thought*. The Catholic University of America Press, Washington, D.C., 1969; John M. Headley, *Tommaso Campanella and the Transformation of the World*, New Jersey, Princeton University Press, Princeton, New Jersey, 1997; D. P. Walker, *Spiritual and Demonic Magic: From Ficino to Campanella*, Kraus Reprint, London, 1969; Maurice Andrieux, *Daily Life in Papal Rome in the Eighteenth Century*, George Allen and Unwin Ltd., London, 1968; Frederick Hammond. *Music & Spectacle in Baroque Rome: Barberinini Patronage under Urban VIII*, Yale University Press, New Haven, 1994; *Source Readings in Music History: The Baroque Era*. Selected and Annotated by Oliver Strunk, W. W. Norton & Co., New York, 1965.

I thank Richard Barz for reading a version of *Kabir* and Gino Moliterno for his encouraging comments on *Tommaso Campanella*. Many thanks go to Kelsey Garlick for editing the manuscript, and Diana Giese for her comments.

www.ingramcontent.com/pod-product-compliance
Lightning Source LLC
Chambersburg PA
CBHW030847090426
42737CB00009B/1134